C000172321

THIS IS THE BEST TRIP

THIS IS
THE BEST TRIP

Chasing the Tangerine Dream

Ian Chisnall

Scratching Shed Publishing Ltd

First published by Scratching Shed Publishing Ltd in 2011
Registered in England & Wales No. 6588772.
Registered office:
47 Street Lane, Leeds, West Yorkshire. LS8 1AP

www.scratchingshedpublishing.co.uk

ISBN 978-0956804310

A catalogue record for this book is available from the British Library.

Typeset in Cheltenham Bold and Palatino

Printed and bound in the United Kingdom by
L.P.P.S.Ltd, Wellingborough, Northants, NN8 3PJ

Acknowledgements

Without that heroic promotion squad of 2009-10 the germ of the idea for this book would never have begun to grow, so a huge thank you to all involved.

To all who played for the club in the Premier League, Ian Holloway and his staff and Matt and the media team, your help and co-operation was much appreciated. Thanks also to Gary Hickson at BBC Radio Lancashire who fed me as rich a diet of Seasiders matches as he possibly could, the Press Association for help with the photographs, plus Phil Caplan and the team at Scratching Shed Publishing Ltd.

To properly proof read a book about Blackpool's exploits in the Premier League you need a Preston North End fanatic. While I know it must have been painful, I am grateful, Trevor! Finally, I must point out that son Craig's professional journalistic advice and wife Jan's endless hours at the computer are the keys to this production getting to the shelves.

Contents

*

Foreword
by Ian Holloway

What can I say about Ian 'Chis' Chisnall? He's just like part of the furniture on matchdays, he pops up everywhere and sometimes I think he's in the squad. And there's another thing. I don't know whether he goes to bed the night before a game because he's always there when we arrive at grounds. In most cases, he's already inspected the pitch when the lads arrive so he can advise them on what studs to wear!

Seriously, Chis does the crucial job of bringing the game live to those thousands of supporters who, for whatever reason, can't get to the match. In my time out of the game I did some summarising on the radio, so I know how difficult a job it is. People in the studio are giving you information all the time in your headphones whilst you're trying your best to describe what you're seeing. It ain't easy and the fact that he's been doing it for over 20 years tells you he knows his business.

I first met Chis at a pre-season friendly at Burscough just

after my appointment. He wasn't working on the day, he just came down to introduce himself and I thought, what about that – the lad has gone out of his way to come all the way to Burscough just to introduce himself. That really impressed me that did… but it was only when I read this book that I realised he lived two miles down the road. Rascal, he didn't tell me that at the time!

As the weeks went by I asked the lads who've been here a while about him - Matt Williams, Phil Horner, Thommo and Brett. They all said the lads trusted him and they're all top blokes so that was good enough for me. Since then we've had some tasty jousts on the microphone. You've got to have a sense of humour to be around this game and Chis has taken some stick from me. One day he called one of my Dutch loan players Marcel Sheep instead of Seip. I just stood there going 'baa, baa', but he carried on with the interview despite everybody wetting themselves.

When I heard about this book I was immediately happy to help out. What Chis has done is given everyone involved in what was an unbelievable season a chance to have a record of it all through his eyes. All of us will have memories to last us forever and whether you agree with the views in the book or not, it doesn't matter. It's there to remind you of a fantastic season and a true fairytale and I wish him all the luck in the world with it.

I have, though, got to finish with just one question.

Chis… what would you have done if we'd defied all the odds, got those couple more vital points and stayed up? That would have knackered your venture, son, wouldn't it?

Ollie
September 2011

*

Blackpool's Season in the Sun

On 22nd May 2009, Blackpool Football Club appointed Ian Holloway as their new manager. Chairman Karl Oyston gave Mr Holloway a clear mission - keep this club in The Championship. The bookmakers had already installed The Seasiders - along with Scunthorpe United - as favourites for relegation.

On 22nd May 2010, the unthinkable happened. Blackpool beat Cardiff City 3-2 at Wembley Stadium to gain promotion to The Premier League with a squad assembled at a fraction of the cost spent by the majority of clubs in their division. There was an outpouring of tangerine joy.

From my privileged position as a member of the BBC Radio Lancashire sports team, I was there to witness that momentous event. This is my match-by-match account of a never to be forgotten season that ended... on 22nd May 2011.

The Best Trip... In Context

After reluctantly hanging up my boots in 1987, I began working for the BBC Radio Lancashire sports team in 1988 as a freelance broadcaster.

Over the years I've covered the highs and lows of our local teams in a wide variety of venues, some well appointed and comfortable, many less so and awkward. During the twenty-plus years it has evolved that Blackpool Football Club has been the one I have become more attached to than the others, a club that has always been close to my heart. It has been a pleasure and a privilege to report on promotions at Wembley and a pain in the pit of the stomach to relay news of relegations.

I've jousted with the whole spectrum of managers from the perfect gentleman that was the late, great Billy Ayre to those who, shall we say, could be a tad more volatile in the heat and emotion of the aftermatch interview. Somehow, I managed to survive the Steve McMahon era unscathed, although I think that was largely down to an extremely liquid late night session in a Bristol hotel before a game at Ashton Gate. Extending the microphone into Gary Megson's face after a cup defeat at home to non-league Hednesford was memorable too. There was a massive - and very vocal - protest from fans outside the old South Stand and a beleaguered Megson was sitting on the floor of the treatment room at the time refusing to move out of the relative safety it provided.

Simon Grayson was a dream to deal with and a pitch-side debrief at Bloomfield early in his reign led to another cameo. As I was halfway through my second question, a seaside seagull deposited what seemed to be its entire load fairly and squarely on my head, but the rookie gaffer just about kept it together despite almost wetting himself with laughter. Tony Parkes was a man of few words in complete contrast to his successor and just where do you start trying to describe Ian Holloway?

Before the end of September in his first season I'd been threatened with being thrown off the pier; by Christmas he was 'going to stick the nut on me' if I used the word 'defeat' again and by the end of a truly remarkable season we shared an emotional hug underneath the Wembley steps. And that moment was to signal where the gaffer's biggest task yet was to begin. Having piloted a promotion that no right-minded person could have foreseen, Ollie's challenge now was two-fold. One: Could he possibly build a squad to keep Pool in the top flight? Two: Could he persuade his chairman to bring in the players he would need to even compete in the million dollar world of the Premier League?

I need to make something clear. My involvement with the football club is on matchdays only, undertaking my assignments for BBC Radio Lancashire. My day job as an Executive Headteacher of a couple of special schools on Merseyside gives me more than enough to do during the week. So, combine that with the fact that I don't live on the Fylde and you'll get the picture that I am distanced from the day-to-day involvement that my colleague and summariser Steve Canavan of *The Blackpool Gazette* has. But even from afar, it was evident that the close season days were turning into weeks with precious little happening on the transfer front. Trialists came and went with no significant announcements of arrivals and with a fortnight to go before the big kick-off, there was a real danger the club wouldn't have enough bodies to fill in a matchday team sheet.

All of this was grist to the mill of those lining up to have a 'pop'. The national press unfurled headlines such as 'Is this the worst team ever to play in The Premier League?' 'Blackpool won't get double figures in points.' 'They'll celebrate if they win a corner'. And whilst much of what was written may have been over the top, I was becoming more fearful by the day that the magnificence of Wembley would turn into a huge embarrassment in the coming season. Then, in true Blackpool fashion and at the eleventh hour, a flurry of signings was announced.

Decent money was paid to bring Craig Cathcart from Manchester United and Chris Basham from Bolton; Israeli international centre-half Dekel Keinan finally sorted all his clearance and paperwork problems, and much travelled striker Marlon Harewood arrived, along with a trio of Frenchmen, Malaury Martin, Ludovic Sylvestre and Elliot Grandin. Not much time to bed the newcomers into a system but at least secretary Matt Williams will be able to fill in a full 18-man team sheet. It's the height of the English summer, but it's time for the club with the smallest budget in Premier League history to do battle with the aristocrats. All aboard the rollercoaster!

Game 1

*

Wigan Athletic
DW Stadium, 14-08-10

This should have been a home fixture but it has been switched because of ground completion work at Bloomfield Road and, living where I do, it's become a home game for me.

I'm up early and just about negotiate a nervous breakfast before leaving home for the short drive to the DW Stadium. I'm there to collect my accreditation by 1230 and I also get the first bad news of the day... I'm working from the TV gantry, complete with the 95 steps! Having lugged the kit up to the roof, I find BBC Manchester already on air with Jimmy Wagg introducing Manchester City at Tottenham in the early game.

The second bad news of the day is only minutes away... my first attempt to connect to the studio wipes our sister station off air. Fortunately the commentary from White Hart Lane had already started and, together with Jimmy and Wigan reporter Paul Rowley, we spend an anxious 45 minutes trying to get both ports to configure. At 1315 we're finally both live together just in time for my two-way with Keith Fletcher in the BBC Radio Lancashire studio. We discuss pies and the fact that come 1700 I will have commentated on Blackpool in all four divisions. Not many will be able to match that.

Back down the steps and the first good news of the day is that injured midfielder Keith Southern informs me that he is to be my summariser. Excellent! The second good news follows almost immediately. I get the chance to meet referee Mark Halsey in reception and wished him well on his return to top flight football after his recovery from a particularly nasty cancer. Then it's back up top for sports boss Gary Hickson to open the programme at 1400. Keith joins me during the usual pre-match duties and, chatting to him off air, it's clear that he's absolutely gutted to be missing the big kick off. The teamsheet arrives and it shows three Blackpool debutants - Craig Cathcart, Elliot Grandin and Marlon Harewood - and before we know it the teams are on the way out. I wish Keith good luck and we're ready to go.

1500   The dream turns to reality. Wigan kick off and skipper Charlie Adam is the first Blackpool player to touch the ball in the Premier League

1502   Brett Ormerod misses two great chances, one of them with an air shot at an open goal

1514   Gary Taylor Fletcher becomes Blackpool's first ever Premier League goal scorer from Harewood's cross
....0-1

1517   Taylor Fletcher has a 'goal' disallowed - incorrectly - for offside and is furious

1537 Marlon Harewood scores after Wigan keeper Chris Kirkland's mistake..0-2

1543 Harewood tucks away number three after Grandin's shot is saved 0-3

1546 The half-time whistle has everyone shaking their head in disbelief. Nobody in the world could have predicted this scoreline

1601 Steve Gohouri has a 'goal' disallowed for Wigan... again incorrectly

1630 Alex Baptiste's cross from the right eludes Kirkland at his near post for a fluke fourth to seal an astonishing win..0-4

1647 At the final whistle the stadium is a sea of tangerine and Keith and I embrace on the gantry before he races off to join the lads

1715 I interview the gaffer pitch side. He is absolutely drained but very proud and even manages to maintain a level-headed approach, pointing out that it won't always be like this...'it's Arsenal away next week'

1725 Gary Taylor Fletcher is delighted to have gone into the record books as Pool's first ever scorer at this level but still hopping mad about the one that was chalked off. TV replays showed him to be clearly on-side but we both end the interview with this stat... BLACKPOOL ARE TOP OF THE PREMIER LEAGUE!!!!!!!!

1736   I climb those steps for the final time to file the interviews before leaving the ground in an absolute daze after what I have just witnessed. Never mind the players, I'm emotionally drained.

1815   Back at home I still can't get my head around an unforgettable afternoon. A large beer from the fridge disappears very quickly, soon to be followed by another. Where are all those knockers who said we wouldn't win a corner, let alone a match?

Wigan Athletic 0 Blackpool 4
- (Taylor-Fletcher, Harewood 2, Baptiste)

Wigan: (4-4-2) Kirkland; Boyce (Stam h-t), Gohouri, Alcaraz, Figueroa; Diame (Thomas, 46), Mc.Carthy, Watson, Moses (McArthur, 72); Boselli, Rodellega

Blackpool: (4-3-3) Gilks; Baptiste, Cathcart, Evatt, Crainey; Adam, Vaughan, Grandin; Ormerod (Sylvestre, 59), Harewood (Basham, 60), Taylor-Fletcher (Euell, 76).

Referee: Mark Halsey.
Attendance: 16,152
Miles travelled: 20

Wednesday August 18th

I receive a call from the studio to inform me that Karl Oyston has stood down as chairman and resigned as a director. He is to remain at the club as acting chief executive in the interim until a new chairman is appointed.

Phil Cunliffe rings me live on air and we discuss and speculate on the impact of the news. I struggle to hide the fact that I'm absolutely staggered by it and am already wondering what effect it will have on Ian Holloway. We didn't have to wait long to find that out...

Thursday August 19th
Ian Holloway gives his reaction...as far as he is concerned
the affair is merely a change of title for Karl and that Mr
Oyston would continue to work with him in player
recruitment. Holloway states that if Karl were to leave the
club, he himself would have to consider his position. Now
that didn't surprise me at all.

Friday August 20th
Stories appear in the national press linking Karl's stepping
down to the fact that he is to be involved in bankruptcy
proceedings at Lancaster County Court. At least something
is beginning to make sense.

Game 2

Arsenal

Emirates Stadium, 21-08-10

This is the fixture I've been dreaming about since Wembley in May: the opportunity to work at the magnificent Emirates Stadium.

There's not a chance of me being late for this one so wife Janis and I leave home on Thursday lunch time. We're heading for North London via son Craig's flat in Sawbridgeworth, Hertfordshire and, would you believe, a day trip across The English Channel to stock up on my wine lake! The journey down country is fine and together with Craig's wife Rachel, we enjoy a fine meal before I retire early. Up at 0530 I'm en route to Dover and, having rammed the car with as many bottles of wine as is humanly possible in France, I even manage to catch an earlier return ferry than scheduled. I'm back in 'Sawbo' for a couple of beers and an excited chat during the meal.

Saturday morning sees a heavily laden Saab journey round the North Circular to second son Dean's girlfriend's apartment in Friern Barnet. What a coincidence... Arsenal tube station is just six stops down the Piccadilly Line! Just before 1130 I'm on the tube enjoying some good banter with the Arsenal fans and I leave them with a request to be kind to us. Little did I know what was to unfold.

I'm outside the ground before 1200. It's an awesome sight and even better from within. Whilst I'm setting up the equipment the advanced party of Blackpool staff arrive and I join secretary Matt Williams, physio Phil Horner, kit man Steve Wales and Keith Southern for a chat in the luxury of the dug-out area. All of us are blown away by the surroundings and the quality of the playing surface. Then it's back to the media suite where lunch is served...grilled salmon with a herb crust, mushroom and pesto with wild rice...just has the edge on the Wigan pies.

At 1320 it's two-way time again with Fletch in the studio and we discuss the splendour of the stadium, the quality of lunch, the regal treatment afforded to the media...and the size of the task in hand. News comes in from Matt that there will be one change to the starting line up from Wigan...Ludovic Sylvestre will play as a holding midfielder on his starting debut, Brett Ormerod dropping down to the bench.

Former Norwich and Ipswich manager Brian Hamilton is in the press box, an old friend from my BBC Radio Merseyside charity football days, and he's happy to do a piece live on air with me. Brian says he fears a little bit for Blackpool today if Arsenal are in the mood...how right he was to be proved.

1501   Under grey North London skies, Arsenal kick off attacking the newly renamed Clock End

1502   Theo Walcott fires in the first of his hat-trick..........1-0

1515 Gary Taylor Fletcher heads Pool's best chance wide from six yards

1531 Blackpool's day turns sour...Ian Evatt brings down Marouanne Chamakh, referee Mike Jones points to the penalty spot (replays show the challenge was outside the box) and sends Evatt off. Andrei Arshavin tucks away the penalty.............................2-0

1537 Ian Holloway shuffles his ten men...Dekel Keinan comes on for a debut in central defence, Sylvestre is sacrificed

1539 Walcott cracks in his second through the legs of Keinan. Half time can't come soon enough. 3-0

1609 Abou Diaby hammers another converting Bacary Sagna's great cross...4-0

1618 Walcott completes a first ever Arsenal hat trick. This could end up in double figures! 5-0

1635 Arsene Wenger shows a bit of compassion and sends on two unknown subs...Fabregas and Van Persie!!!!!

1637 Chamakh heads his first goal for Arsenal from Van Persie's corner 6-0

1649 The final whistle blows and the torture is over. Blackpool fans give their team a standing ovation... Charlie Adam departs with Cesc Fabregas' shirt

1717 An extremely helpful steward allows me to interview the gaffer pitch side. Ollie's upset about the penalty and sending-off incident but realistic and not too downcast. Honest as ever he shows genuine relief to have only conceded six in the circumstances.

1740 I have a last look around the stadium, thank the staff for their help during the day and head back to the tube. There are still hundreds of smiling Blackpool faces in evidence on the way.

1850 Having reclaimed the car we're off home. Thankfully, the motorways are clear of traffic problems but full of Pool fans who, despite the crushing defeat, have enjoyed a dream day out in the capital.

2205 We arrive back just in time for *Match of the Day...* Pool are first on for the second successive week. What a fantastic day!

Arsenal 6 Blackpool 0

(Walcott 3, Arshavin, Diaby, Chamakh) -

Arsenal: (4-3-3) Almunia: Sagna, Song, Vermaelen, Clichy: Diaby, Wilshere (Fabregas, 62), Rosicky; Walcott (Vela, 66), Arshavin (Van Persie, 62), Chamakh.

Blackpool: (4-4-2) Gilks: Baptiste, Cathcart, Evatt, Crainey: Sylvestre (Keinan,37), Adam, Vaughan, Grandin; Taylor Fletcher (Ormerod 57), Harewood (Demontagnac 57)

Referee: Mike Jones
Attendance: 60,032

Miles travelled: 440
Total Miles: 460

Game 3

*

MK Dons

Stadium MK, Carling Cup round 3, 24-08-10

A cup draw that nobody really wanted…another long journey with the prospect of a much changed team. Still, it will be another new venue for the club and for me. Not trusting the traffic through the Midlands I'm on the road just before 1500 and, with help from the car radio, I decide that the A50 will be a better route to the M1 than via Birmingham. It proves a decent decision and I'm outside the impressive Stadium MK at 1800 after only one minor wrong turn through the infamous Milton Keynes roundabouts.

Then it's a footballing first for me. After collecting accreditation I am directed to the main entrance of The Hilton Hotel which doubles up as the Main Stand. Never before have I entered a ground via hotel reception.

With the equipment set up and checked I proceed down to pitch level where the team has just arrived. Chatting with Charlie Adam, Stephen Crainey and Matt Williams it's clear that Crains is still being ribbed by the lads about Theo Walcott's display. The Scot held his hand up and admitted that Walcott was unbelievably rapid and predicted that plenty of other full backs would get the same treatment. It emerged that there were to be ten changes to the line up from Saturday at Arsenal including four debutant starters on a night when Ian Holloway is elsewhere looking at potential transfer targets leaving Steve Thompson in charge.

The programme begins on the night of a three-way commentary split and when the teamsheets arrive they reveal that Ludovic Sylvestre is the only man to start from Saturday. There are club debut starts for keeper Mark Halstead, Dekel Keinan, Chris Basham and 18-year-old second year scholar Tom Barkhuizen. Regular summariser Steve Canavan joins me in the commentary box and we reflect on that fabulous day at Arsenal as we wait for kick-off.

1945   Referee Tony Bates gets the game underway

1945 and 59sec
       Sam Baldock fires MKDons ahead with what proves
       to be the only goal of the half.....................................1-0

2050   Ishmel Demontagnac's shot comes back off the post
       and keeper and Brett Ormerod tucks it away. Muted
       celebrations as the linesman's flag rules it out.

2052   Neal Eardley's right wing cross is finished from close
       range by Ormerod. This one does count.................1-1

2054   Jermaine Easter strolls through the Pool defence to
       beat Halstead 2-1

2056   Easter repeats the dose after swapping passes with
       Baldock...3-1

2058 Sylvestre's free kick rounds off a remarkable period of four goals in six minutes 3-2

2108: 2112: 2116
Big hitters Taylor Fletcher, Adam and Grandin appear from the bench

2125 Brett is pushed in the back for a penalty, hastily despatched by Adam 3-3

2131 Brett has another effort ruled out by the linesman .....

2134 Danny Coid ensures there will be extra time by clearing off the line from Peter Leven

2201 Substitute Lewis Guy gets beyond Blackpool to stroke home what proved to be the winner............4-3

2220 I interview Craig Cathcart on Northern Ireland call-up. The young centreback is a man of few words

2230 Matt Gilks comes out to give his reaction to his Scottish call-up and the interview couldn't have been more different. Gillo, a born and bred Englishman, clarifies his qualification through his grandparents and jokes that he's going to buy a kilt and learn to play the bagpipes

2238 Steve Thompson has been pitch-side and on the phone to Ian Hollway for 25 minutes. At last he's able to be interviewed and feels his young side were a touch unfortunate

2252 I leave Stadium MK with the unappetising thought

of 165 motorway miles to be negotiated. Driving into my garage at 0150 on Wednesday morning, I'm quietly questioning my sanity

---

MK Dons 4 Blackpool 3 (after extra-time)
(Baldock, Easter 2, Guy) - (Ormerod, Sylvestre, Adam, pen)

MKDons: (4-4-2) Martin; Woodards, O'Hanlon, Kuou-Doumbe, Lewington; Chadwick, Hamann (Guy, 64), Leven, Balanta (Carrington, 89); Easter, Baldock (Ibhere, 69)

Blackpool: (4-3-3) Halstead; Eardley, Keinan, Edwards, Coid; Husband (Adam, 72), Basham, Sylvestre (Grandin, 76); Barkhuizen (Taylor Fletcher, 68), Ormerod, Demontagnac

Referee: Tony Bates
Attendance: 7,458

Miles Travelled: 330
Total Miles: 790

Friday August 27th:
Luke Varney joins Pool on a season long loan from Derby.

Game 4

Fulham

Bloomfield Road, 28-08-10

Premier League football finally arrives at Bloomfield Road and the new East Stand opens…and where am I? On my way to Bramall Lane for Sheffield Utd against Preston North End. It's one of only two Pool games that I'll miss before the turn of the year and although I've known about it for a couple of months, now that the big day is here, I'm gutted not to be heading for the seaside.

As I head out of the village, it's a struggle to force the car eastwards and not due north, but I always enjoy going over the tops to Sheffield and the traffic was decent. I'm parked up outside Bramall Lane at 1315. Whilst collecting my press pass I am the subject of attempted abuse from the North End journos. I'm on the TV gantry and with all checks completed, it's down to the press room.

Pie and peas…very nice too…and, during the course of my lunch, I field a number of calls from people wondering why I'm not at Bloomfield Road. That simply adds to my frustration. With the programme underway I listen eagerly to Gary Hunt bringing team news from Blackpool. Ian Evatt is back from his ban, Brett Ormerod returns for Sylvestre and there's a debut for new boy Varney in place of the injured Marlon Harewood.

1535   My commentary on an eminently forgettable first half at Sheffield is interrupted by news of a goal at the seaside...Bobby Zamora has headed Fulham into a lead they would hold until half time....................0-1

1546   My game drifts to the break goalless.

1626   The studio informs me of another goal at Blackpool...YES! Luke Varney's shot comes back off keeper David Stockdale only for John Pantsil to turn it into his own net..1-1

1629   French debutant Jean Calve hammers the match winner for Sheffield United past Andrew Lonergan from 35 yards

1631   I'm told to cross to Bloomfield again...the noise tells me Pool are ahead through a debut goal for Varney, drilling home Brett's pass..2-1

1644   Tension as the studio inform me of another goal...Dickson Etuhu's close-range finish levels things up at ....2 - 2

1649   The final whistle here signals another away defeat for Preston and it's also finished in a draw at the seaside in front of England boss Fabio Capello. That will do!

31

1705   I interview a frustrated Darren Ferguson before heading back to the car

1720   As I'm driving out of Sheffield Ian Holloway is being interviewed on Sports Report. Realistic as ever he is disappointed not to have won but admits he would have taken a point if offered it before the match.

1915   I arrive home and attack the fridge again!

Blackpool 2 Fulham 2
(Pantsil o.g., Varney) - (Zamora, Etuhu)

Blackpool: (4-3-3) Gilks; Baptiste, Evatt (Eardley, 64) Cathcart, Crainey; Adam, Vaughan, Grandin; Ormerod, Varney, Taylor-Fletcher

Fulham: (4-4-2) Stockdale; Kelly, Hangeland, Hughes, Pantsil; Murphy (Gera, 80) Duff (Greening, 85) Etuhu, Davies; Zamora (Dempsey, 59) Dembele

Referee: Michael Oliver
Attendance: 15,529

Miles Travelled: 210
Total Miles: 1000

Tuesday August 31st (Transfer Deadline Day)
Matt Phillips, a winger, arrives from Wycombe for an initial fee of £325,000. DJ Campbell FINALLY signs from Leicester in the hour before 1800.

Wednesday September 1st
Australian international David Carney was also signed before the deadline from FC Twente Enschede

Thursday September 2nd
Ian Holloway adds to his goalkeeping cover by bringing in free agent Richard Kingson, Ghana's World Cup stopper

Friday September 10th

As Janis and I are travelling to the North East prior to Pool's game at Newcastle, I'm contacted by the studio with some devastating news. Youth team coach and former BBC Radio Lancashire summariser Gary Parkinson is critically ill in hospital after suffering a massive stroke.

Parky and I became good friends in the three years he worked alongside me and he was a regular travelling companion before his return to work in football. I felt physically sick for a few hours as I tried to come to terms with such a dreadful bombshell.

It's so ironic that we're en route to the North East...Parky's birthplace. Jan and I can't stop thinking about the horrific news and all our thoughts are with him, Debs and the family. This is the guy who regularly had my boys in tears of laughter in the car on their way to away games with his tales from football dressing rooms over his career. Come on Parky...you were always a fighter!

Game 5

*

Newcastle United

St James Park, 11-09-10

The morning dawns bright and dry and I enjoy a bracing walk out to the Roker Lighthouse before tackling a mountainous breakfast. After checking out we take the scenic run along the coast via Tynemouth and enjoy all the preparations for next week's Great North Run.

Arriving in Newcastle from a completely unfamiliar direction, I manage two laps of the city centre before locating the car park for St James. Janis accompanies me to the stadium before heading off into the city and I'm in the media suite early enough to watch *Football Focus* coming live from the ground. I set up the equipment whilst England Test spinner Graeme Swann is being interviewed on the pitch. Mick Lowes from BBC Newcastle informs me that Swann is due up at the radio point later and I relish the prospect of doing a piece with him.

The two-way with Keith Fletcher is not its usual light-hearted affair, but it proves useful in enabling me to broadcast the good wishes of all at the radio station to Debs and the rest of Parky's family. When the team bus arrives, I manage a chat with physio Phil Horner and Steve Thompson. They'd been to see Parky on the Friday morning but the news is bleak. Brett and Keith tell me how much they want to win this game for their stricken mate.

The team news shows the need for enforced changes: Alex Baptiste (hand) Gary Taylor-Fletcher (calf) and Craig Cathcart (illness) all miss out: Neal Eardley, Dekel Keinan and DJ Campbell replace them. Graeme Swann arrives at the press point and agrees to do an interview. Swann is in town to watch his beloved Newcastle and what a top bloke he proves. I was determined to steer well clear of the Pakistani betting scandal but Swanny was more than happy to bring it up and it makes for a really good interview. Our studio are delighted with the piece.

1512   Steve Harper saves as DJ fluffs a one on one chance in what's been a very bright Blackpool start

1526   Mike Williamson hits the post for Newcastle

1531   Matt Gilks pulls off the first in a string of wonder saves to deny Kevin Nolan

1544   Almost 50,000 gasp as Alan Smith fells Luke Varney in the box. Charlie Adam strokes home the spot kick to give Blackpool a deserved half-time lead. The skipper then grabs a T-shirt with '4 Parky' written on it and holds it aloft..0-1

1616   Gilks continues his heroics to deny a clean through Joey Barton

1643   Pool's brilliant keeper repels Andy Carroll's drive with his feet…nothing's going past him today!

1644   As the Geordies push forward, Charlie carries the ball 65 yards before finding DJ. A crisp 20 yard left footer gives him a debut goal and Blackpool three points 0-2

1705   Ian Holloway dedicates the victory to Parky and Debs and sends love from all at the club. He is 'astonished' by the level of performance in the circumstances on his 'proudest day in football'.

1715   DJ, wearing a huge ice pack on his right leg, comes to the interview room and explains how difficult it was to prepare for the game in the tragic context. He talks then of his special relationship with Charlie and that he has set himself a goals target - but won't tell us! Work completed I head for the car park wearing a broad grin and enjoy clear roads on the drive home. The radio brings coverage of an astonishing game at Turf Moor where Burnley come from 1-3 down late in the day to beat Preston 4-3.

2000   Guess what, that fridge is due for a bashing again!

Newcastle 0 Blackpool 2
- (Adam, pen. Campbell)

Newcastle: (4-4-2) Harper; Perch, Coloccini, Williamson, Enrique; Routledge (Ameobi, 80), Smith (Lovenkrands, 62), Barton, Guttierez (Ben Arfa,72); Nolan, Carroll

Blackpool: Gilks; Eardley, Keinan, Evatt, Crainey; Adam, Vaughan, Grandin (Carney, 84); Ormerod (Harewood, 65), Campbell, Varney (Southern, 84)

Referee: Lee Mason
Attendance: 49,597

Miles Travelled: 380
Total Miles: 1380

Game 6

*

Chelsea

Stamford Bridge, 19-09-10

It's the back end of a double header for me so it's not a weekend away but a major day trip. Advance warning has allowed me to let the train take the strain so I'm in the hands of Sir Richard Branson after a very wet drive to Runcorn. I park the car in a street simply named 'Holloway' and I'm nice and early on the platform for the 09.54 to Euston. Its trouble free and courtesy of the Northern and District underground lines, I'm outside Stamford Bridge at 1330.

I greet Owen Oyston and President Valeri Belokon on my way round to the media entrance in the East Stand. I've arranged to meet Craig and Rach and together we head for a pre- match beer in an adjacent Irish Bar. With Manchester United playing Liverpool on the TV it seems as though the whole population of Dublin and West London are in there! Then I head back to the ground for an excellent press room lunch - chicken korma - and prepare to pick up the programme for Radio Lancs at 1545.

Immediately prior to going live I discuss the teamsheet with Steve Canavan - Alex Baptiste is fit again and included at the back of a midfield diamond to the exclusion of Brett Ormerod. With Keith Southern also fit, both Steve and I wonder whether this system will work.

1600   Chelsea kick off and keep the ball for a full minute until Dekel Keinan at last gets a Pool touch in conceding a corner on the champions left.

1601   Drogba's delivery is flicked on by Ivanovich and Salomon Kalou fires home from close range..........1-0

1611   Drogba powers into the box and Florent Malouda has a simple tap-in from his skipper's low cross...2-0

1620   Ashley Cole torments Neal Eardley yet again before a pull back to Drogba. His 18-yard effort flies past Matt Gilks right hand, with the keeper on his way to his left. Replays show Drogba's shot cannoned away off Ian Evatt's backside 3-0

1640   Elliot Grandin loses the ball cheaply in midfield and in an instant it is switched to Kalou on the right. His cross is volleyed sweetly home by Malouda..........4-0

1646   Merciful relief as Mark Clattenberg signals half-time. Talk in the press room is will it be eight or nine and I am genuinely fearing an embarrassment in front of the eyes of the nation.

1701   The teams reappear with Gary Taylor Fletcher replacing Eardley and Baptiste happy to be restored to right back.

1715   Taylor-Fletcher is thwarted by Petr Cech's tip over

1716   Marlon Harewood and Brett Ormerod replace Luke
       Varney and Elliot Grandin. Pool are much better

1730   Alex Baptiste clears off the line from Ashley Cole

1734   Harewood shoots into the side netting and from
       their vantage point the outstanding seaside
       supporters think it's a goal. Wild - but short lived-
       celebrations!

1743   Drogba blazes over just before the final whistle and
       Pool survive a real hiding. The players are given a
       standing ovation by the travelling fans.

1815   Carlo Ancelotti heaps praise on Blackpool for their
       positive reaction. 'They played well after half time'.

1825   The gaffer arrives after taking an age doing TV. He
       admitted he'd got the formation wrong and said he
       was hurt by it but, in what is becoming a recurring
       theme, says he is proud of the players response in
       second half.

1835   Interview filed, gear packed for home, I bump into
       John Motson. I remind him of a wet afternoon at
       Wycombe Wanderers (Loakes Park) where I marked
       him in a charity football match in 1988. Being Motty,
       he remembered all the details!

1940   I arrive outside Euston and decide on a pint in the
       pub opposite the station, where friends and
       Blackpool diehards Nikki and Paul join me. Other
       smiling happy Blackpool fans arrive and time passes
       quickly before my train at 2121.

This Is The Best Trip...

2121   The train departs bang on time and it's another
        painless journey home.

0045   So tired am I on making it home I don't even have a
        drink! Another fabulous day out.

Chelsea 4 Blackpool 0
(Kalou, Malouda 2, Drogba) -

Chelsea: (4-4-2) Cech; Ferreira, Alex (Bruma, 70), Ivanovich, Cole; Ramires (Zhirkov, 74) Essien, Obe Mikel (Benayoun, 76), Malouda: Kalou, Drogba

Blackpool: (4-1-3-2) Gilks; Eardley (Taylor-Fletcher, 45), Evatt, Keinan, Crainey; Baptiste; Vaughan, Adam, Grandin (Harewood, 61); Campbell, Varney (Ormerod, 61)

Referee: Mark Clattenberg
Attendance: 41,761

Miles Travelled: 440
Total Miles: 1,820

Game 7

*

Blackburn Rovers

Bloomfield Road, 25-09-10

The studio have changed my fixture so it's not a first visit to the seaside quite yet...I'm literally being sent to Coventry. Gary Hickson was apologetic about it but he's the boss and he needs me to commentate on this one.

At least I have a travelling companion...I pick up Allan Smart at Junction 27 on the M6 and chatting football, jobs and more football, the journey passes really quickly. We arrive at The Ricoh Arena in time to watch the early game on TV...Manchester City versus Chelsea...and help ourselves to lunch, chicken balti pie and peas.

Our programme is being presented live from Bloomfield Road and team news from there is in soon after 1400. Craig Cathcart is fit and returns to the defence in a team with four out and out strikers...DJ, Marlon Harewood, Brett and GTF..in it. The gaffer is definitely going for it! Smartie and I speculate on Preston's poor start to the season but both have a sneaking feeling they might get a result today.

1520   Preston, who started this game rock bottom of the

league, are more than holding their own as news comes into my headphones of a goal at Blackpool. I freeze as I am informed that Charlie Adam has scored...AN OWN GOAL...0-1

1535 Coventry keeper Kieron Westwood parries Sean St.Ledger's header and Billy Jones puts Preston ahead from close range

1544 A terrific strike from Iain Hume doubles North End's lead as the half time whistle blows at the seaside with no change to the scoreline.

1616 Aron Gunnarson hauls Coventry back into the game, hooking over Andy Lonergan from 12 yards. Game on.

1641 Preston are hanging on really well when I am told that Matt Phillips has come off the bench to score a late equalizer with his first touch in the Premier League. Magic...a point will do for me.................1-1

1650 Preston's much needed victory is confirmed but just as Allan Smart and I wrap up the commentary, the studio tells me Brett Emerton has won it for Blackburn in stoppage time. Gutted!.....................1-2

1710 A very relieved Darren Ferguson appears for interview and as we wait for Billy Jones to appear, there's a classic comedy moment. Not for nothing is big Preston striker Jon Parkin known as 'The Beast'...he's a huge man. Parkin had poked in what he thought was a clinching third goal close to the end, only to see it ruled out for offside. As big Jon emerged from the dressing room he was asked if he was offside. Probably just came the reply..'but my f...ing fat arse would be still have been on-side.' Priceless!

1725 Duties completed, Smartie and I head for the car and the M6. Neither of us are great '606' fans with Robbie Savage spoiling some excellent analytical comments by intimidating some of the callers so we mull over the day's results up and down the country

1910 Drop my passenger off and drive to my local, The Windmill in Parbold, on the way home. Won't be quite so keen to watch *Match Of The Day* tonight!

Blackpool 1 Blackburn 2
(Phillips) - (Adam o.g. Emerton)

Blackpool: (4-3-3) Gilks; Eardley (Phillips, 84) Evatt, Cathcart, Crainey; Adam, Vaughan, Taylor-Fletcher; Ormerod (Varney, 65) Harewood (Grandin, 66) Campbell

Blackburn: (4-4-2) Robinson; Salgado, Nelsen, Samba, Givet; El Hadji Diouf, Jones, Nzonzi (Andrews, 66), Pederson; Kalinic (Benjani, 71), Mam Biram Diouf (Emerton, 46)

Referee: Mike Dean
Attendance: 15,901

Miles Travelled: 250
Total Miles: 2,070

Game 8

*

Liverpool

Anfield, 03-10-10

After almost 25 years of working on Merseyside surrounded by Koppites it's no wonder I'm an excited boy when I wake early. Plans don't go as they should...it's Ryder Cup weekend and I'm up with the lark to watch the golf...but not for the first time this weekend, horrible weather means there will be no play until 1330.

It's a filthy morning in the North West too and I encounter many flooded sections of the East Lancs Road into Liverpool. Problem number two arises when I reach the car park to be advised by a half-drowned steward that there is no pass for me. I ring Radio Merseyside's Gary Flintoff who sorts things out from the ground. A very helpful steward...Jimmy...meets me at The Shankly Gates with a pass and I return to park, this time successfully, at Stanley Park.

The monsoon abates and I am able to walk to the ground without getting a real drenching. Gary is having lunch as I bestow many thanks for sorting out the car parking situation. I do the usual set up and test operations with the ISDN before returning to the press room. Chicken and mushroom pie on the menu...received and consumed with thanks before Anfield legend Tommy Smith appears.

Having skippered Tommy's Sunday League side to two league titles it's great to catch up with him again. He wastes no time in telling me that this is the worst Liverpool side he has ever seen but when the teamsheet arrives it bears the names Gerrard, Torres, Cole, Kuyt and Reina et al. I still have a feeling of foreboding about what may happen during the course of the next few hours.

Back up at the press point I do a two-way with Gary Flintoff on BBC Merseyside, my rugby league employers, before the Lancashire studio hands over to me at 1445 to take the programme up to kick-off. Steve Canavan is alongside me and with the help of a couple of Holloway interviews, the time roars by. Steve and I both take time out from talking to let the listeners enjoy the Kop's rendition of 'You'll Never Walk Alone'...spine chilling!

1501   Mike Jones gets us underway with Blackpool, all in white, attacking The Kop

1510   Fernando Torres has a groin problem and is replaced by David Ngog

1515   DJ is inches away from Neal Eardley's cross

1520   Craig Cathcart gives way to Dekel Keinan with a niggle in his back

1526   A brilliant Charlie Adam pass is collected by Luke Varney who cuts inside Glen Johnson only to be brought down. Penalty!

1529   Charlie goes to Pepe Reina's left and despite the keeper getting a hand to it, it's in. BLACKPOOL LEAD AT ANFIELD! 0-1

1546   Blackpool's domination is rewarded by a second goal. Great work from DJ and GTF who slides in Luke Varney to beat both the offside flag and Reina 0-2

1547   Half time...the ground rises to applaud The Seasiders off...what a sight and sound

1602   More disruption for Blackpool as Neal Eardley does not re-appear. Young Matt Phillips, a forward by trade, is asked to play at right back

1611   A free kick awarded for a seemingly non-existent hand ball is taken quickly by Gerrard and the big Greek, Sotiros Kyrgiakos, heads Liverpool back into the game 1-2

1616   Liverpool are buzzing at last and Joe Cole shoots wide when he should really have made it 2-2

1620   Keith Southern replaces Grandin and Blackpool look tight and composed again

1648   Stoppage time almost over as Matt Gilks performs heroics to beat away a goal bound header from Kyrgiakos. The whistle blows and a momentous victory is savoured by 3000 almost delirious fans.

1705   Lovely moment in the dressing room corridor. Most of the players had swapped shirts as they left the pitch but Gillo was still out there receiving some treatment from Phil Horner after a late knock and the pair eventually left the pitch alone. As we waited for the interviews, Pepe Reina left the home changing room, purple keepers shirt in hand. He knocked and was admitted to the away changing room where he swapped shirts with Gillo. Typical of the man and typical of this great club.

1708   I interview a manager who is emotional and 'chuffed as a badger.' The gaffer dedicates the win to his late dad who worshipped everything to do with what he described as the greatest football club in the world...Liverpool.

1715   As you would imagine, there are no shortage of players willing to be interviewed...Luke Varney, fresh with his swapped Steven Gerrard shirt, and Ian Evatt oblige

1735   Interviews filed it's a look around the almost deserted stadium. I have to pinch myself to believe this. Having stood on the Kop during my university years watching the club not only dominate the domestic game but Europe as well, I have just witnessed my team come to Anfield in the best league in the world and beat Liverpool. Not only that, they thoroughly deserved to...somebody wake me up! As you will have gathered by now, I have an urgent appointment at home with a large, cold can of beer and then another....

Liverpool 1 Blackpool 2
(Kyrgiakos) - (Adam, pen. Varney)

Liverpool: (4-5-1) Reina; Johnson, Kyrgiakos, Skrtl, Carragher; Kuyt, Poulsen (Jovanovic, 60) Meireles, Cole (Maxi, 88); Gerrard: Torres (Ngog, 10)

Blackpool: (4-3-3) Gilks; Eardley (Phillips, 46), Evatt, Cathcart (Keinan, 20), Crainey; Adam, Vaughan, Grandin (Southern, 63); Taylor-Fletcher, Campbell, Varney

Referee: Mike Jones
Attendance: 43,156

Miles Travelled: 40
Total Miles: 2,110

Game 9

*

Manchester City

Bloomfield Road, 17-10-10

I'm finally destined for Bloomfield Road with the season two months old...but even this isn't via the usual route. We're in home town Barrow for a family party so wife Janis is to drop me off en-route south. Through secretary Matt and a couple of phone calls, Liverpool based Danny Coid has agreed to bring me home after the game. It's a brisk walk beside the Irish Sea, a late breakfast and we're underway around 1130. Bits and bobs of traffic mean a couple of minor detours but I'm dropped off outside the ground just after 1330.

So it's off to see Matt and collect programmes from the home games I've missed as well as today's. The Mersey derby is on TV and GTF, Keith and Coidy are all in Matt's office watching. I take some stick from Coidy about the lift home arrangements - the lads say he's got taxi signs all over his car! Time passes quickly talking to the stewards and some fans who I obviously haven't yet seen this season before Gary Hickson and Micky Mellon arrive. I already have the team news for them, Blackpool fielding the exact starting eleven from Anfield. Gary opens the programme at 1530 as a terrific atmosphere builds and before I know it, the teams are on their way out. Show time! Paupers v Princes.

1620   Matt Gilks tips an Adam Johnson thunderbolt over the bar, but that came on the break as Blackpool are the better team without really troubling Joe Hart in the City goal. Charlie Adam and David Vaughan are dictating the game from midfield.

1645   An enthralling first half somehow finishes goalless and Pool receive a standing ovation as they go off.

1719   Varney and GTF get DJ in one against one with Joe Hart but the Pool striker curls wide of the post.

1721   David Silva replaces Emmanuel Adebayor in the change that was to win the match for City. Tevez moves up top and Silva plays in the hole.

1723   Silva crosses for Tevez to touch City ahead from close range. Instantly, TV replays show the Argentinian is clearly offside 0-1

1734   Wayne Bridge gives away a cheap free kick 40 yards from goal and substitute Marlon Harewood deftly heads in Charlie's delivery...1-1

1735   Bridge attempts to atone for his error by charging 70 yards at the heart of the Blackpool defence. Vaughan stops him and as Ian Evatt moves to clear the danger he appears to be fouled by Tevez. No whistle though and Tevez's shot is deflected beyond Gillo by Craig Cathcart. Hard to bear! 1-2

1745   The brilliant David Silva curls in a wonder strike
       from 15 yards and surely it's all over 1-3

1749   Blackpool stick at it and from Charlie's corner, GTF
       tucks away Luke Varney's shot. Surely not! 2-3

1750   Phil Dowd allows one more attack but time runs out
       for a valiant Blackpool in a clash of epic proportions.
       For me, Pool's performance has surpassed anything
       I've seen for a very long time – including Wembley,
       Forest and Anfield.

1820   Having crossed the pitch for interviews, Steve
       Canavan and I are stationed in Matt's office where
       we can hear the gaffer going absolutely ballistic in
       the dressing room. Matt has been dispatched to the
       referee's room and he returns with news that Phil
       Dowd will see Ollie when the due 45 minute cooling
       off period from the end of the game is up.

1825   An incandescent Holloway emerges from the
       dressing room but is clearly in no state to fulfil his Sky
       and BBC TV commitments. Matt ushers him into the
       room where Steve and I are and we listen in silence as
       more steam is let off whilst Matt attempts to becalm
       him.

1835   Sky's deadline is drawing close and the gaffer
       reluctantly agrees to go to the TV room.

1840   Ollie and minder Matt leave the TV room and head
       straight for the referee's room. The door closes and
       nobody sees sight of them until1920.

This Is The Best Trip...

1855   Steve and I interview Neal Eardley – in case that's all we get! Eards has already seen the video and knows that City's first two goals should not have stood but says it was a fantastic performance

1920   Manager and minder snaffled by *Match of the Day*.

1935   Finally, the pair are available to me. The gaffer is still seething about the lack of technology available to the officials, but manages enough self control to give me a broadcastable six minutes worth of his feelings.

1945   I emerge to see Danny Coid still waiting for me in the tunnel. I am hugely apologetic and embarrassed - this would happen on the only day I have ever imposed myself on a player's generosity.

1951   Risking the wrath of groundsman Stan, I charge straight across the pitch to file the interviews.

2001   At last I'm able to end Coidy's long wait and we leave the ground.

Blackpool 2 Manchester City 3
(Harewood, Taylor-Fletcher) - (Tevez 2, Silva)

Blackpool: (4-3-3) Gilks; Eardley (Phillips, 76) Evatt, Cathcart, Crainey; Adam, Vaughan, Grandin (Harewood, 66); Campbell, Taylor-Fletcher, Varney

Manchester City: (4-4-2) Hart; Boateng (Richards, 76) Lescott, Company, Bridge; A Johnson (Viera, 85), De Jong, Barry, Milner; Adebayor (Silva, 65) Tevez

Referee: Phil Dowd
Attendance: 16,116

Miles Travelled: 90
Total Miles: 2,200

Game 10

*

Birmingham City
St Andrews, 23-10-10

Matchday sees me wake around 0845 …at least 1,200 miles from Birmingham. It's my last ever October half-term break and we're in Albufeira on Portugal's Algarve coast in the middle of a week in the sun. For obvious reasons I need the weather to be spot on today to keep my mind off where I should be and a brilliant blue sky is already in evidence. Pretty soon my Blackpool T-shirt brings attention from a Blues supporter around the pool and we chat about the afternoon's prospects before the early Sky game is shown on the TV at the poolside bar.

I pay only cursory attention to Spurs and Everton contesting a 1-1 draw. A habitual check on the mobile phone almost induces heart failure…a message from sports boss Gary Hickson checking that I'm OK to do the 1320 two-way with Keith Fletcher. Has Gary forgotten I'm abroad and not sent anyone else to do the game?

I'm in the process of analysing my options in replying to him when my torture is ended. A second message comes through apologising for the mistake. Thank God for that!

This Is The Best Trip...

It's still baking hot so I deliberately opt for sunbathing, a swim or two and a snooze rather than scouring the resort to find the match being piped around Europe on TV. All of a sudden it's 1635 and it's a quick dash to the room and BBC's *Final Score*....

1637   Birmingham 2 Blackpool 0. BBC 's Ivan Gaskell describes Pool as 'completely out of sorts and unlikely to score if they played all night'

1650   Further bad news... Charlie, after a mental block to gift City the second goal, went off injured. Sounds like a good one to miss!

1715   Jan and I head off for a long walk around the resort. A couple of pints of ice cold San Miguel help ease the pain, as will a steak and a bottle of red.

2225   Pull up a chair ready for *Match of the Day*. TV highlights are sometimes deceptive but a typically forthright Ian Holloway confirms that his side got what they deserved.

Birmingham 2 Blackpool 0
(Ridgewell, Zigic) -

Birmingham: (4-4-2) Foster; Carr, Johnson, Ridgewell, Dann; Larsson, Ferguson, Fahey (Bowyer, 66) Hleb (Murphy, 74); O'Connor (Derbyshire, 83) Zigic

Blackpool: (4-3-3) Gilks; Eardley, Evatt, Cathcart, Crainey; Adam (Southern, 66) Vaughan, Taylor-Fletcher; Campbell, Harewood (Phillips, 66) Varney (Ormerod, 76)

Referee: Anthony Taylor
Attendance: 26,850

Game 11

*

West Bromwich Albion

Bloomfield Road, 01-11-10

For the first time this season, matchday coincides with a working day for me at both schools. The 'day job' is relatively busy being the first day back after half term, but I've managed to get home by about 1700. Double checking that the kit is all packed it's off north at 1720 to arrive at the ground 1815 ish. It's a Sky game so car parking arrangements see me in the newly acquired West car park and thankfully the rain abates as I walk to the stadium to set up the kit for Gary Hickson to pick up the programme at 1900.

All week there's been a major doubt about Charlie's fitness after having 4 stitches in an ankle wound, so I wander over to the dressing room area to find the man himself in the corridor. 'Are you fit Chas?' 'No'. 'Are you playing Chas?' 'Yes'. So the side shows just one change ... Elliot Grandin in for Marlon Harewood. Gary arrives and with the help again of former Baggie Micky Mellon, we chat things through until kick off at 2000. In every respect, this is a big, big game.

This Is The Best Trip...

2000   Michael Oliver get us underway ... blindly ignorant of the night he was set to have!

2008   Matt Gilks saves well from Simon Cox before the action quickly reaches boiling point.

2010   Charlie's pin point pass isolates DJ with Albion centre back Pablo Ibanez in the box. Ibanez brings him down and it's a clear penalty, awarded instantly. But then mayhem – West Brom looked to have other covering defenders but it's a red card for a distraught Ibanez. Charlie squeezes the penalty just under Scott Carson 1-0

2014   Steven Reid replaces the sacrificed Cox and Yousuf Mulumbu sees yellow for dissent.

2029   Chilean right back Gonzala Jara has a brainstorm and dives into a completely unnecessary two footed lunge at Luke Varney in the corner. No doubt this time about the validity of the red card and West Brom will have to play for over an hour with nine!

2033   Albion's intentions are clear as their other striker Marc Antoine Fortune is replaced by Graham Dorrans, a midfielder. It's a keeper, four at the back, four in midfield formation and West Brom are excellent at it until half-time.

2111   Craig Cathcart has to be at full stretch to divert a Jerome Thomas effort wide before Ian Holloway changes things. Wide men Matt Phillips and David Carney replace defenders Cathcart and Eardley.

2120 Phew, relief at last as Luke Varney slides in Pool's second after excellent work from Vaughan and Grandin. Surely, that should be that........................2-0

2128 Dekel Keinan replaces Varney as Blackpool look to shut up shop.

2142 West Brom have been a credit and after substitute Giles Barnes is denied by Gilks, Youssuf Mulumbu curls in a magnificent goal. Game back on. 2-1

2148 Fourth official Chris Foy holds aloft the board to signify four minutes of stoppage time, just as Steven Reid blazes over from eight yards. The nine men couldn't equalize…could they?

2150 DJ,Grandin and Charlie all waste chances to clinch that elusive home win.

2151 Bloomfield Road breathes a huge sigh of relief as the whistle blows to signal a first home top flight victory since April 1971.

2210 I interview a delighted Luke Varney who states he is so happy at the seaside that he'd like to make his loan move permanent.

2215 Ian Evatt is next up and emphasises the importance of the three points and how difficult it was to play against nine men.

2220 Ian Holloway arrives and promptly disagrees with my first question. Even by his standards, a four minutes and ten second response is outstanding. He stresses reality, asks for more patience from the fans and is clearly bouncing to have thirteen points from the first ten games. It's a great interview, with the 'ugly woman' again getting a mention.

2234 Interviews all filed, it's off for a very wet drive home. All of a sudden, I realise I haven't eaten anything since 1330 so I'm hungry...but happy.

Blackpool 2 West Brom 1
(Adam, pen. Varney) - (Mulumbu)

Blackpool: (4-3-3) Gilks; Eardley (Phillips, 57), Evatt, Cathcart, (Carney, 57) Crainey; Adam, Vaughan, Grandin: Campbell, Varney (Keinan, 70), Taylor-Fletcher

Referee: Michael Oliver
Attendance: 15,210

West Brom: (4-4-2) Carson; Jara, Ibanez, Tamas, Shorey; Brunt. Mulumbu, Scharner, Thomas (Barnes, 69) Cox (Reid,14) Fortune (Dorrans,33)

Miles Travelled: 90
Total Miles: 2,290

Thursday November 4th
A disturbing story has been brewing of late regarding a dispute over unpaid bonuses between Charlie Adam, his agent and the club.

Details are sketchy and, quite rightly, the full facts are not revealed in public. But what is clear is that there is a major obstacle to the resolution of the situation, so much so that the case is to be heard in a London court room today. From what has been reported, it appears that the issue centres around a clause that would have given Charlie a bonus if the club were not relegated from The Championship in the 2009-10 season. Karl Oyston's stance on behalf of the football club was that this particular clause was not now relevant because the players earned an even bigger bonus by being promoted. Some may see it as a technicality and, from a distance, surely the matter could have been sorted in-house. But to court it went...and there was one potentially unthinkable outcome.

Should all the aspects of the matter be proven successfully in the favour of the club's talisman skipper and figurehead, Blackpool could have been deemed to be in breach of contract. Charlie Adam could then walk away from his contractual situation right now and the club would not receive a penny. Don't go there!

Friday November 5th
The Premier League announce that the case has been heard at their tribunal and that the judgement would be made public on November 24th. Now don't they say a week is a long time in politics?...almost three weeks to sweat on what could be a possible season shattering announcement! Unfair on all parties in my opinion.

Game 12

*

Everton
Bloomfield Road, 06-11-10

A glorious November day for a match I've been looking forward to since the fixtures were released. It's the Merseyside connection again and day to day contact with so many Evertonians has led to some great banter in the build-up. I desperately need the lads to come with up a performance and a result so I can hold my head high at work on Monday.

I've got shopping duties so it's off to the seaside nice and early. I'm parked up and in position by 1130 and am chatting to groundsman Stan when my mobile sounds. It's youngest son Dean with news that he's landed a principal role in *Shrek: The Musical* to open on Drury Lane next spring. He's over the moon and together we agree that it might be a good omen for the day. Then it's off to the club shop and a walk along the promenade before getting back to the ground at about 1300 where I wander round to the main stand as I need to see secretary Matt. I knock on his office door but find it locked and turn away back into the corridor.

Instantly the door is flung open - it's the gaffer with a

bollocking for me. 'F...ing hell Chizzers, I didn't have you down for breaking and entering. You better come in without smashing the door down. Gordon Bennett!!!' He's laughing his head off as I apologise profusely before I get more abuse from Matt with Coidy and GTF greatly amused witnessing the cameo.

Having learned that Keith is to start in place of Elliot Grandin, I retreat back to the East Stand. That's a significant change as Blackpool's starting XI will be entirely British ... I wonder when the last Premier League line up was without a foreign born player? Steve Canavan joins me at the point as we are doing full commentary for BBC Radio Merseyside and Jon Lowe in the studio counts me down for a 1459 start.

1500 Andre Marriner, taking charge of a Blackpool match for the first time since that memorable May afternoon at Wembley, gets proceedings underway.

1509 A clumsy Everton challenge gives Blackpool a free kick 25 yards out. As the whole of the ground waits for Charlie's hammer, Neal Eardley curls it round the wall to beat Tim Howard for the perfect 22nd birthday present 1-0

1513 After a quickly taken free kick on the left, Sylvain Distin clips in a perfect cross and Tim Cahill thumps in a header for his 50th Premier League goal.........1-1

1540 Seamus Coleman shoots just wide after a half hour of Everton domination.

1546 Blackpool are relieved to go in at half-time on level terms.

1605   After DJ and GTF have shots blocked, David Vaughan scores at the second attempt 2-1

1607   Another Coleman raid down the right ends with a low shot straight at Matt Gilks who proceeds to dive over it in a horrible moment for a keeper who has been in outstanding form ....2 - 2

1623   Gilks goes some way to atoning for his error by keeping out Steven Pienaar – who knows he's missed a sitter.

1627   Substitute Louis Saha is in behind Ian Evatt and one against one with Gillo. He beats the keeper but rolls wide. What an escape!

1646   Blackpool sub Marlon Harewood has the ball in the net but the 'winner' is ruled out for a push on Phil Jagielka. TV replays show Pool were hard done by.

1715   It's a point apiece after another epic encounter and the players from both sides go off to thunderous applause. A beaming Ian Holloway comes to the interview room and entertains us for almost 10 minutes. He is well pleased with his point and his players. 'I'd pay to watch my boys...they were fantastic against a very good football team.'

1725   Goal scorer David Vaughan is reluctantly brought for interview and the quietly spoken Welshman, voted man of the match, talks us through the feelings inside a very happy dressing room.

1745   Equipment de-rigged, its time for home on another

thoroughly enjoyable day. I can't wait for work on
Monday.

Blackpool 2 Everton 2
(Eardley, Vaughan) - (Cahill, Coleman)

Blackpool: (4-3-3) Gilks; Eardley,
Evatt, Cathcart, Crainey: Adam,
Southern (Phillips, 60) Vaughan;
Campbell, Taylor-Fletcher
(Grandin, 74) Varney (Harewood,
74)

Referee: Andre Marriner
Attendance: 16,094

Everton: (4-4-2) Howard; Neville,
Distin, Jagielka, Baines; Heitinga
(Beckford, 77) Coleman, Arteta,
Pienaar (Bilyaletdinov, 75); Cahill,
Yakubu (Saha, 60)

Miles Travelled: 90
Total Miles: 2,380

Game 13

*

Aston Villa
Villa Park, 10-11-10

This is a carefully selected day off from work for me and I'm hoping for some decent weather to combine a round of golf with my trip to England's second city. The day dawns cold but clear and I'm on the tee at Leyland at 0905. Very wet conditions and a covering of autumn leaves sees me lose at least half a dozen golf balls but I enjoy it nevertheless. A quick shower, home for a light lunch and off to battle the motorways...and battle proves an appropriate expression. The journey starts badly with heavy traffic on the M58 and it takes me 35 minutes, instead of the usual eight or nine, to get to the M6. All is well then until the daily congestion between junctions 12 and 9 but I'm safely parked up and on my way to the ground at 1745. Twenty minutes later, equipment set up and checked, I'm back in the press lounge paying serious attention to the chicken balti when secretary Matt arrives. He tips me the wink about the team news...oh my goodness, ten changes from Saturday's team with only Keith Southern starting again. A shiver of fear runs through me on two counts...the most immediate with regard to tonight's score line: in the longer term a fine looks certain (Wolves were found to be in breach of Premier League rule E20 for a similar selection last season.) As soon as the news is released at 1845 the press box and lounge are agog with questions being fired at the Blackpool contingent from all sides. Little wonder that the time to kick off time disappears into the very cold West Midlands night air!

1945   Villa kick off attacking their famous Holte End but, right from the outset, Pool look bright

1958   Marlon Harewood scoops a great chance wide after brilliant approach play by debutant Matt Phillips.

2013   Stewart Downing's shot from the edge of the box takes a huge deflection off Dekel Keinan to leave keeper Richard Kingson stranded.............................1-0

2030   Patient Blackpool passing eventually sees a cute back heel from Phillips leave Harewood through with only Brad Friedel to beat and the former Villa man coolly slots an equaliser....................................1-1

2103   Keinan is slow to rise to a right wing cross and Nathan Delfouneso soars above him to head home. Referee Anthony Taylor rules it out immediately indicating a push. Replays confirm Pool have got away with one!

2104   Delfouneso is clean through the middle and guides his shot to Kingson's right...2-1

2111   Ian Holloway plans a triple substitution with Charlie, DJ and Luke all stripped and ready for action. Just as play stops, Dekel Keinan goes down with an ankle injury and eventually walks painfully towards the touch line for attention. Changes put on hold and Ian Evatt emerges to warm up.

2114   Keinan comes back on but clearly can't continue. Blackpool take a ridiculous three minutes before Ian Evatt can replace him. Varney gets the track suit back on and DJ joins Charlie in the action.

2133   DJ breaks his two month goal drought when his low shot is deflected over Friedel by James Collins......2-2

2135   Pool despite being heroic on the night had always been vulnerable in the air and from Downing's late corner, Collins powers in the winner.......................3-2

2140   Four minutes of stoppage time can't yield a third equalizer and both sides are cheered to the rafters as they leave the pitch.

2201   The gaffer emerges from the TV interviews and is beaming with pride as he describes his players efforts and defends his team selection. Little did I know this was to be the calm before the storm.

2210   Steve Canavan and I wait for the players to arrive as the boss is interviewed in the tunnel by BBC Radio Five Live's Pat Murphy. Even from our proximity it's clear that the interview is not going well as the level of Ian Holloway's voice rises and rises. As Steve and I interview Keith Southern, Matt and an irate gaffer leave the scene to face the written press. Even more anger was to follow in the media theatre and it later emerges that Holloway has threatened to resign if either he or the club are punished with regard to the team selection.

2243   I leave Brookvale Road car park to head home. Radio Five Live play parts of their interview with the manager and the station is inundated with callers ringing in with their support for the gaffer's decision. The phone in makes the journey home race by and I'm home after a very full...and interesting... day and I'm pouring a Bushmills at 12.15.

Aston Villa 3 Blackpool 2
(Downing, Delfouneso, Collins) - (Harewood, Campbell)

Aston Villa: (4-4-2) Friedel; L. Young, Dunne, Collins, Warnock; Albrighton, Bannan (Lichaj, 89) Clark, Downing; Delfouneso (Agbonlahor, 64), A. Young	Blackpool: (4-3-3) Kingson; Basham, Edwards, Keinan (Evatt, 76) Carney; Euell (Adam, 68) Southern, Sylvestre; Ormerod, Harewood (Campbell, 73) Phillips
Referee: Anthony Taylor Attendance: 34,330	Miles Travelled: 240 Total Miles: 2,620

Game 14

*

West Ham United

Upton Park, 13-11-10

A long-awaited fixture for two reasons…I've never been to Upton Park and it's that time of year again…my birthday weekend. I've travelled in style for proper pre-match preparation…Virgin trains first class from Wigan on the Friday (tickets won at Pool secretary Matt's cricket dinner!) Top hotel too, the Hilton at Canary Wharf, family curry in Brick Lane…this is living! No problem getting to sleep and pleasant dreams of Pool picking up points…zzz…zzz

Match day dawns grey and cold in London's Docklands. Following an excellent breakfast I stroll down to the steam room and sauna thinking I've really arrived on the scene. Charlie Adam eat your heart out…this is one BBC reporter preparing as if he's playing! I even manage a stroll around the impressively re-developed Millwall Dock area before catching the DLR 1205 service to Bow Church. A walk to Bow Road and the District Line gets me to Upton Park by 1245. It's too early for the club and the press door remains firmly shut until 1255. Then it's in and up to the gods to set up the equipment...Upton Park is all I thought it would be...an old fashioned, proper football stadium. Kevin Hand from BBC London collars me for a two-way before I head back downstairs for a coffee and a sandwich. I ring Matt for confirmation that it's the 'A' team back for what is a big game for both sides...yes,11 changes from midweek. Phil Cunliffe is presenting our programme and we dip in and out before kick off time. Both sides and a big crowd, including both Chisnall boys, observe the Remembrance Day silence brilliantly and we're off.

1517   After a lively start, West Ham are forced into an early change - Kieron Dyer has to give way to Pablo Barreira

1525   David Vaughan fires wide after a really good run

1528   Big home shout for a penalty as Craig Cathcart blocks from Victor Obinna

1547   Half time arrives without a goal - that in itself is almost miraculous

1601   Matt Gilks doesn't re-appear and Richard Kingson takes over in goal

1605   Luis Boa-Morte shoots wide - a bad miss

1609   Charlie tries his party piece shooting from fully 50 yards and inside his own half and Robert Green is relieved to see it land on the top of his net

1623   DJ has to limp off and Marlon Harewood gets a terrific reception at another of his former clubs

1626   Harewood turns in from close range but the flag is
       up. Replays show Marlon to be clearly on side and
       the goal should have stood.

1627   Hammers sub Carlton Cole hits a post under
       challenge from Ian Evatt

1630   The miss of the match belongs to an embarrassed
       GTF, ballooning over from six yards after
       Blackpool's best move of the match. If that doesn't
       go in its bound to finish goalless ...

1646   And it does!

1705   I'm in the players tunnel and with the gaffer already
       in the TV room, I get the chance to knock off a quick
       interview with Luke 'Reg' Varney.

1710   Ian Holloway appears and he's well pleased with his
       point. He also heaps praise on West Ham, what they
       stand for in the game and how an under pressure
       Avram Grant conducts himself.

1717   Ian Evatt completes the media duties and he too is
       delighted, particularly with the clean sheet. Matt
       Gilks is walking OK and says he heard something
       click in his knee whilst taking a goal kick. He will
       have a scan on Monday.

1730   All done and ready to go. It's a quarter of a mile to
       the tube and not a single car moves in the grid-lock
       outside

1740   I catch the tube with Stewart and Alec from the

club's media team. There's loads of good natured banter on the train from both sets of supporters.

1810   I'm back at the hotel where there's a Peroni on ice waiting. This is the life...maybe I'll do this for all the away trips!

West Ham 0 Blackpool 0

West Ham: (4-4-2) Green; Jacobsen, Upson, Gabbidon, Ilunga; Dyer (Barreira, 17) Parker, Noble, Boa-Morte (Cole, 71); Obinna, Picquionne (McCarthy, 81)

Referee: Kevin Friend
Attendance: 31,194

Blackpool: (4-3-3) Gilks (Kingson, 45); Eardley, Evatt, Cathcart, Crainey; Adam, Vaughan, Grandin (Phillips, 58); Taylor-Fletcher, Campbell (Harewood, 66) Varney

Miles Travelled: 460
Total Miles: 3,080

Tuesday November 16th

It emerges that Matt Gilks has fractured his knee cap and will need surgery. He evidently incurred the injury kicking the ball at a goal kick after 25 minutes and played on with it until half-time. Incredible! You have to feel sorry for Gillo - playing out of his skin, called up by Scotland and now this. I also worry about Blackpool's goalkeeping situation - with, of course, the greatest respect to Richard Kingson.

Game 15

*

Wolverhampton Wanderers
Bloomfield Road, 20-11-10

At the risk of repeating myself, this is yet another significant day for me. It's eldest son Craig's 30th birthday and Jan and I have arranged a surprise party for later this evening. But the day won't be anything if Blackpool don't win - or at least get something this afternoon. Dean is here too and it's just like old times as the three of us set off nice and early for the match. By 1245 the equipment is set up and tested and I stroll round to the main stand and tunnel area.

At this time on matchday there might be two or three stewards and club officials around but as I walk in there is a group of at least a dozen crowding around the door to reception. I ask what is going on but the normally out-going staff are very tight lipped and suddenly the reason is obvious. A group of young men arrive and are immediately ushered upstairs...one of whom is the future King of England. In the week that Prince William announced his intention to marry next year, he is here at Bloomfield Road with his mates from RAF Valley on a stag do...UNBELIEVABLE.

To matters more urgent – there's been a doubt about Charlie since his injury playing for Scotland, so when he drops into the media office, it's my turn to begin the well rehearsed sequence –'Are you fit Chas?' 'No' - 'Are you playing Chas?' ... 'Yes' Stephen Crainey's next in and I'm able to congratulate him on his international appearance – top lad, he's so appreciative. The team shows just the four strikers ... Marlon, DJ, Luke and a home debut for Matt Phillips – do you think Ollie is going for it? Once again Phil Cunliffe is presenting but I'd been advised that news of the royal presence was strictly under wraps so I follow instructions and say nothing. Then the Prince takes his seat and the cameras were all over him like a rash! So when it was open season I announce that the most talked about and famous man in the world this week is here at Bloomfield Road. You could sense the whole ground is buzzing as the news spreads and an already cracking atmosphere is ratcheted up another notch. Kick off time can't come soon enough.

1502   Luke Varney chest controls Ian Evatt's pass, cuts inside Kevin Foley and blasts a wonder of a big dipper over Marcus Hahneman from 30 yards. It's a world class and right royal opener which has the young prince on his feet 1-0

1529   Wolves replace Foley by Milijas and continue to look the better team

1537   Ian Evatt ranges forward to test Hahneman

1543   It's big Evo again winning a corner after the Wolves goalkeeper denies him

1545   Luke Varney nods down David Vaughan's corner for
Marlon Harewood to earn a half time lead 2-0

1617   Nenad Milijas smashes against the post from 20
yards – a real let off for Pool

1621   GTF and Ludovic Sylvestre replace Phillips and
Harewood

1633   Richard Kingson saves a close range drive from
substitute Ebanks-Blake

1643   Evatt is hurt executing a trade mark block. Having
had treatment under that ludicrous rule, he's off the
field as the resulting corner comes in, Kevin Doyle,
who would have been Evatt's man, heads Elokobi's
cross past Kingson 2-1

1651   Kingson scrambles an extra-time cross over the bar
and as soon as the corner is taken, the whistle blows
on a hugely important three points for Blackpool

1703   Matt brings Ian Holloway into the office for the
interviews. He admits his side have been a touch
fortunate to win, but astutely points out that this
may have been the first time this season that has
happened. The gaffer, a massive royalist, oozes pride
as he talks about meeting Prince William and jokes
that he warned him to 'leave our women alone'.

1723   I manage to catch Luke Varney between various TV
interviews to talk about 'that' goal. Modestly, 'Reg'
would rather talk about another three points and
how much he is enjoying his football

1740   Just packing the gear up when Craig and Dean return…from the pub! Back home by 1830 where some of the family are already installed. The 'surprise' element of the day is diminishing, but part one – the collection of three points – is safely accomplished. Here's to an enjoyable evening…but, little did I know it, what with covering other fixtures and some horrendously inclement weather, this would be my last look at Blackpool until after Christmas!

Blackpool 2 Wolves 1
(Varney, Harewood) - (Doyle)

Blackpool: (4-2-4) Kingson; Eardley, Evatt, Cathcart, Crainey (Carney, 90); Adam,Vaughan; Phillips (Sylvestre, 64) Campbell, Harewood (Taylor-Fletcher, 64) Varney

Wolves: (4-4-2) Hahneman; Foley (Milijas, 29) Berra, Stearman, Elokobi, Henry (Fletcher, 60) Mancienne, Jones, Jarvis; Doyle, Hunt (Ebanks-Blake, 46)

Referee: Mark Clattenberg
Attendance: 15,922

Miles Travelled: 90
Total Miles: 3,170

Wednesday November 24th
The day of judgement in the Charlie bonus fiasco that threatens Ian Holloway's plans. The announcement is heart stopping and the committee finds in favour of Charlie with regard to the bonus payment and judge that it should be honoured by the club. But the worst case scenario is thankfully avoided when the context of the situation is taken into account…Blackpool Football Club were found not to be in breach of contract. What a result, what a relief…Charlie 1 Mr. Oyston 1. Both parties celebrated their respective victories…now, can we get back to the job in hand please!

Game 16

Bolton Wanderers
Reebok Stadium, 27-11-10

Another difficult match day for me…I'm heading to Greater Manchester, but not to the Reebok. I've been despatched to Old Trafford where United are to take on Blackburn. BBC Radio Lancashire's commentary agreement with Rovers fell through and on that basis, Gary Hickson has re-allocated Andy Bayes to the Reebok - lucky sod! Still, I suppose there could be worse places to broadcast from than the Theatre of Dreams.

I set off early fearing that Christmas shopping traffic heading for the Trafford Centre may be an issue but my worries are unfounded and I'm safely parked up by 1230. A wind straight from Siberia cuts through me as I get out of the car – this is going to be a cold one. The press lounge at Old Trafford is its typically cosmopolitan self – there are radio crews there from France, Sweden and Norway as well as our national big hitters. After setting up the equipment it's a welcome and warming lamb curry for lunch watching Villa being second best to Arsenal on the TV. The whisper from the Rovers press boys is that Morten Gamst Pederson won't play – a blow for Sam and the Norwegian radio crew. The teams arrive just after two – a certain Mr. Rooney starts for United and I hear from Bayesy at Bolton that Elliot Grandin is back for Pool in place of Matt Phillips with GTF replacing the injured Marlon Harewood. Regular pieces with the studio pass the pre-kick off minutes as another massive crowd builds up at Old Trafford.

1502 It's a flying start for United as Berbatov glances in Nani's cross

1523 Following a glorious pass from Rooney and Ji Sung Park gets number two

1525 Pascal Chimbonda turns blind with an intended back pass only to find Berbatov who clips past Robinson

1526 Never mind all the excitement here, Ian Evatt heads Blackpool in front from Grandin's corner. I'm on my feet in the press box 0-1

1604 The slaughter of the innocent continues as Dimitar Berbatov celebrates a hat-trick with a crisp right footer

1605 Even before I've finished telling the listeners it's four, Nani cuts in from the right and smashes home another

1614 Another Blackpool corner at the Reebok and this time Luke Varney finishes Grandin's delivery. Could Pool hang on? 0-2

1619   Back here, Berbatov hasn't finished yet as the
       Stretford End net bulges with number six

1626   Red hot Bulgar Berbatov grabs five in the game with
       a close range shot

1630   Bad news in the headphones...Bolton sub Martin
       Petrov hammers a Wanderers reply. It's going to be a
       long quarter of an hour now 1-2

1640   Lively Rovers substitute Josh Morris crosses for
       Chris Samba to register what won't really be a
       consolation

1646   I can hardly bear to listen as Mark Davies ties things
       up at the Reebok. Blow it now referee, I'll take a
       point 2-2

1715   Full-time here on a drubbing...and thankfully it's all
       over at Bolton. I'd have taken a point at the start of
       today.

1735   Eventually Big Sam appears for the press conference.
       He's realistic and says it's one to forget...what
       nobody forsees is that this would be his penultimate
       game in charge before his ludicrous sacking.

1810   I manage to catch a bit of Ian Holloway's interview
       whilst negotiating traffic in Trafford Park. He says
       it's the best his team in tangerine have played and
       calls for Prince William to give all his players a
       knighthood. Steady gaffer!

Bolton 2 Blackpool 2
(Petrov, Davies) - (Evatt, Varney)

Bolton: (4-4-2) Jaaskelainen; Ricketts, Cahill, Knight, Robinson; Lee (Moreno, 60) M. Davies, Muamba (Klasnic, 70) Taylor (Petrov, 60); K.Davies, Elmander	Blackpool: (4-3-3) Kingson; Eardley, Evatt, Cathcart, Crainey; Adam,Vaughan, Grandin (Carney, 88); Taylor-Fletcher (Ormerod, 84) Campbell, Varney (Southern, 86)
Referee: Mike Dean Attendance: 25,851	Miles Travelled 90 Total Miles: 3,260

Saturday December 4th

After days of freezing temperatures, a tasty home fixture against League leaders Manchester United is lost to the weather. Groundsman Stan Raby and his team were always up against the ravages of the elements. Despite strenuous efforts, the game didn't stand a chance. Sub zero nights meant this sell-out fixture had to be re-scheduled for a midweek evening. With United still very much involved in the Champions League, that will prove a challenge in itself and more headaches for secretary Matt. Is this a good postponement? Blackpool had evidently been excellent at Bolton but Manchester United were awesome in spanking Blackburn for seven.

The weather is also giving the gaffer, Thommo and Stephen McPhee a different set of problems. Squires Gate, totally exposed to the wilds of the weather at the best of times, has been a skating rink for much of the week and finding suitable alternative training venues is becoming a real issue as the freeze continues. A test for the staff then ... everyone knows what footballers are like when they're not playing and if they can't train as they would wish, the lads will be a nightmare to handle.

Game 17

*

Stoke City

Britannia Stadium, 11-12-10

Another difficult matchday for me ... instead of travelling south to Staffordshire, I'm heading north to Blackpool's big rivals, Preston North End but not until after an early morning workout. Wife Janis is off to Standish to buy the Christmas tree so I take the chance of a power walk from the M6 junction back home. Not bad, I cover the four and a bit miles in just under the hour and freshly showered and breakfasted, I'm off to Deepdale at 1215. After a trouble free journey, I'm greeted by the car park steward as a 'Tangerine donkey-lasher' ... and a Merry Christmas to you too! He advises me to park in space number four and says that's how many Stoke will get this afternoon. I respond with a wide grin and ask him 'what league is that in?' I share lunch with North End General Manager, Ben Rhodes who lets me know that Preston are unchanged. Radio Suffolk's Brenner Woolley joins us and he knows the Ipswich line up so we share information and generally have a catch up before climbing the steps to the commentary point. Gary opens the show and its just ten minutes before Andy Bayes brings news that Blackpool are unchanged at Stoke in what will certainly be the biggest physical challenge yet for Ian Holloway's men. Although I don't make public knowledge of it to the Preston journos, I fear for Blackpool this afternoon.

1520   Billy Jones loops a header for Preston onto the Ipswich bar ... a chance against the run of play as the Tractor Boys dominate the half.

1540   Bad news from afar – Charlie Adam picks up a yellow card and will be suspended for next week's big game against Spurs.

1546   Andy Bayes reports the half-time whistle and he and Steve Canavan suggest that Blackpool have slightly shaded a goalless first half and before he finishes his report, the entertainment (or lack of it) before my eyes reaches the same stage with a similar score line.

1601   Both sides are ready to re-start at Deepdale with the action already underway at Stoke.

1604   Bayesy lights up my afternoon....DJ Campbell diverts Charlie's shot in from close range YES!.....0-1

1607   Iain Hume cracks Preston in front.

1608   Agony in the ear holes as I sit squirming waiting for the whistle at Stoke.

1651   I'm on my feet punching the air as Bayesy calls time and Pool have another astonishing and unlikely victory. Even the Preston stewards are impressed!

1653   Huge relief for Darren Ferguson as North End cling on to three crucial points against what turned out to be a very poor Ipswich.

1720   After visiting Trevor Hemmings' hospitality box to see his father Sir Alex, the Preston boss comes across for the interview and as expected, he's visibly delighted and, as ever, extremely courteous.

1740   Kit all packed away and the first voice I hear back at the car is Ian Holloway on Radio Five Live. He is purring about what he describes as his team's best performance yet.

1805   I'm just about home by the time Radio Lancashire play the gaffer's interview. He refuses to let Andy Bayes single out any players but reinforces his delight with all concerned. Me ... I'm off to the pub for a celebration beer.

Stoke 0 Blackpool 1
- (Campbell)

Stoke City: (4-4-2) Begovic; Wilkinson, Shawcross, Huth, Collins; Pennant (Tuncay, 70) Whitehead, Delap, Etherington; Fuller, Jones (Walters, 70)

Referee: Anthony Taylor
Attendance: 26,879

Blackpool: (4-3-3) Kingson; Eardley, Cathcart, Evatt, Crainey; Adam, Vaughan, Grandin (Phillips, 81); Taylor-Fletcher, Campbell, Varney

Miles Travelled: 40
Total Miles: 3,300

Saturday December 19th

Everyone has been buzzing in the wake of that fantastic result in The Potteries and Sunday can't come quick enough. Tottenham are having a season to remember as well, making the most of their Champions League experience and with the way both teams approach any game, this is possibly the most eagerly awaited fixture yet. Certainly the TV schedulers didn't take too much persuading to select this one for early afternoon viewing. The weather had relented too and despite a forecast of light snow, the ground staff are confident they'll get the show on.

Light snow ... it never snows on the Fylde does it? ... and even when it does, the salt charged sea breezes see it disappear as soon as it hits the deck. But not on black - or should it be white - Friday! Five hours of heavy snow in the evening brought the north west of England to a standstill. Villages, including mine in Newburgh, were cut off and for the first time in many, many years, Blackpool and the Fylde copped it too. But there was still a confidence that the snow would clear ... as it always does ... and that the Spurs game would go ahead. Then the temperatures dropped and the white carpet was encrusted with frost. While the club were confident the pitch would be ready, the real concern centred upon the seats, concourses and access to Bloomfield Road.

Marooned in my West Lancashire village, I'm faced with an unusual dilemma. I'm glued to the radio whilst digging a way out of my drive. If this game survives and I'm snowed in there could be a suicide to report, but then a dose of sanity prevailed. A meeting of all agencies reached an early conclusion that a postponement was the only sensible course of action. At least the digging can slow down now - I thought I was auditioning for the role of 'Tunnel King' in *The Great Escape*. I hope these weather induced games off are not going to damage Blackpool's survival chances.

This Is The Best Trip...

Sunday December 26th

No Christmas cheer at the seaside and it's not funny now! Desperate for this game against Liverpool to go ahead, the club have invested in sheets to cover the pitch and brought in hot air blowers. These measures seemed to be doing the trick until the latest quirk of the fates conspired against Pool. Groundsman Stan even disturbed his Christmas Day to go down and check that all was well at the ground and was immediately alarmed by the silence as he got inside. Instead of the dull drone of the generators driving the blowers there wasn't a sound to be heard.

It later transpired that the plunging temperatures had frozen the diesel in the generators and what chance of getting them repaired late on Christmas Day? Matchday morning's decision was yet another easy one to make and a bitter blow to take. Three of the highest profile home games for Blackpool have now had to be postponed as the winter freeze continues. Tickets for the scheduled visit of Liverpool today were sold out months ago, as most Boxing Day fixtures are, so now the re-arranged games against today's opponents, Manchester United and Tottenham Hotspur will all have to be midweek evening kick-offs.

Meanwhile, all of this inactivity is seeing other clubs steal a march on Pool and even the most naïve of supporters know that games in hand are nowhere near as valuable as points on the board. Pool are going to face a fixture log-jam and the gaffer bemoans the loss of games and that that he still can't find anywhere where his squad can do any meaningful training. Boxing Day without football is worse than Christmas Day without turkey.

Game 18

*

Sunderland

Stadium of Light, 29-12-10

After days of scrutinising every conceivable weather forecast, overnight rain has accelerated the long awaited thaw and with the car packed with extra clothes, the spade, wellies etc., eldest son Craig and I are off bright and early at 0920. Traffic bulletins don't bring any bad news and but for some patchy fog around Scotch Corner, the journey to the North East goes well. We're parked up at 1215 and walk around this magnificent stadium.

On the way back to the car we meet Radio Five Live's Peter Slater - he was to play a crucial role later in the day. Craig departed to a friendly local hostelry and I entered the ground and set up the equipment. The players arrive and I'm down to the tunnel area to exchange compliments of the season. Steve Bruce is talking to Matt and he wishes me all the best – what a nice guy he seems. Charlie is serving his suspension – at last – and I learn that Ludovic Sylvestre is to replace him in the only change. Christmas dinner is then served in the press room ... there's so much that Steve Canavan actually leaves some food – unheard of! The programme starts slightly before the schedule at 1400 – and I'm still on my way back from the loo. But with all our Premier League and Championship teams in action, the pre kick off hour flies by and we're ready to rumble.

1511   Darren Bent cuts in from the left and slides his shot wide when he should really have done much better - a sign of things to come.

1514   Bent, Danny Welbeck and most notably Asamoah Gyan continue to miss a host of gilt-edged chances

1519   Elliot Grandin has to limp out of the action with a hamstring problem and it's Matt Phillips and not Keith Southern who replaces him

1531   Sunderland are forced into a change too - Titus Bramble replacing a limping Nedum Onuoha

1538   DJ Campbell fires Pool's best chance of the half wide after a brilliant run by Phillips

1544   Gyan is forced wide by a combination of Richard Kingson and Craig Cathcart and can only find the side netting

1547   Half-time. Heaven knows how it can be goalless

1607   Pool force an early corner and skipper Vaughan rolls it back for Eardley to cross. Big Evo flicks it on and DJ belts Blackpool ahead 0-1

1621   Craig Cathcart should have made it two but plants his free header wide

1639   Darren Bent's 25 yard free kick clatters back off the
        bar and I begin to wonder if it's ever going to go in
        for the 'Mackems'.

1647   90 minutes on the clock and Matt Phillips refuses to
        waste time going into the corner and I almost curse
        in commentary. Instead he dances past two, crosses
        low and DJ converts via the under-side of the bar.
        Game over...0-2

1651   The players receive a rapturous ovation from 3,000
        ecstatic travelling fans

1720   Ian Holloway finally gets to me after endless TV
        interviews. He admits his side rode their luck but is
        beaming with happiness and usual pride. Correctly,
        he praises his side for not letting the recent
        postponements disrupt their form and confidence.

1735   Match winner Campbell completes the interviews
        after getting a bear hug from former boss Bruce. He
        says the dressing room is 'bouncing'.

1750   With interviews filed, I'm joined by a joyous Craig
        and that man Peter Slater again. He offers to lead us
        away from the grid-locked traffic back to the A19.
        It's an offer which ultimately saves us at least half
        an hour as we follow him through the back streets.
        At one stage, I think I've been dropped into a scene
        from 'The Italian Job!'. We're on the A19 and en
        route to a family party in Barrow in no time. Thanks
        Pete! Plenty to smile about on the way home until
        we get to Scotch Corner. The fog is thick and driving
        isn't easy for the next hour or so but finally the M6

This Is The Best Trip...

looms and we make the family party in Barrow by 2030. Guess what...I'll have to celebrate with a beer...or two or three especially as Craig stuns the family with the news of wife Rachel's pregnancy. Wonderful!

Sunderland 0 Blackpool 2
- (Campbell 2)

Sunderland: (4-4-2) Gordon; El Mohamady, Onuoha (Bramble, 31) Ferdinand, Bardsley; Henderson, Cattermole, Meyler (Richardson, 58) Welbeck; Bent, Gyan (Malbranque, 66)

Blackpool: (4-3-3) Kingson; Eardley, Evatt, Cathcart, Crainey: Vaughan, Grandin (Phillips, 19) Sylvestre (Southern, 79); Taylor-Fletcher (Carney, 79), Campbell, Varney

Referee: Andre Marriner
Attendance: 42,892

Miles Travelled: 380
Total Miles: 3,680

Game 19

*

Manchester City

City of Manchester Stadium, 01-01-11

And a Happy New Year! Yet again, I've been looking forward to this one since the release of the fixtures, this time with very good reason. My impending visit to the City of Manchester Stadium will complete my set of working at every ground in The Premier League.

That was one reason to have a very circumspect New Years Eve ... couple of pints, nice meal with friends and family and bed just after 0115. Craig is still up north and we have a light breakfast and head for East Manchester at 1120. Traffic is light, the journey is straightforward and suddenly the stadium appears...if it's as good inside as it looks from the outside, I'm in for a treat. Wow, it's magnificent and so too is the sumptuous hospitality which Craig and I enjoy in the subterranean media suite. Five Live's John Murray is in the press room along with former Blackpool player Tony Rodwell and we lunch watching the early game on TV - West Brom v Manchester United.

I'm upstairs setting up the equipment when the players arrive and I'm off down to pitch level to wish them a Happy

This Is The Best Trip...

New Year. I take particular delight in telling Charlie about my fabulous Christmas present - a trip to the Old Firm game in Glasgow tomorrow! He calls me a jammy ...... and tells me to have a great day. He also confirms he is back after suspension in a straight swap for the injured Elliot Grandin. Armed with that information I'm in good shape for the programme to open at 1400 with Andy Bayes in the chair. He begins the show with an emotional review of 2010 ... and all that drama. A few two- ways with all the reporters and the big crowd is ready bang on 1500.

1501   Charlie marks his return with a blind attempted back pass which sends Carlos Tevez through on goal ... only for the City skipper to drag his shot wide.

1507   More comedy defending gives Tevez another chance, this time the Argentinian blazes over.

1514   Joe Hart saves brilliantly from GTF's 15-yard curler

1533   Tevez is again denied by Richard Kingson

1534   From the resulting corner, Ian Evatt's headed clearance only finds Adam Johnson just inside the box. His first time shot nicks Stephen Crainey and flies past an unsighted Kingson.................................1-0

1535   City win possession straight from the kick off and Ya Ya Toure cuts into the box. Luke Varney throws in a reckless and needless tackle and Mark Clattenberg has no option other than to award a penalty

1536   Carlos Tevez pulls his low shot wide of Kingson's right-hand post. The silence says it all.

1540 DJ puts GTF clear but he doesn't realize how much time he has to turn and shoot and wastes the opportunity with a backheel

1546 Half-time and Blackpool are still in it ... just!

1601 Matt Phillips replaces Ludovic Sylvestre at half-time - it must be tactical.

1602 Phillips has already skinned Serbian international Alexsander Kolarov twice as Blackpool look to get the ball out to the substitute at every opportunity

1614 Kolarov is replaced by the more experienced Pablo Zabaleta

1619 Blackpool are the better side as James Milner comes on for David Silva

1626 A terrific block from Charlie stops Tevez in his tracks

1629 GTF gives way to Brett as Tevez hooks wide from close range

1633 Hart makes a terrific save to push away a Neal Eardley thunderbolt in what would prove to be the game's last chance

1648 City complete their double over Pool – but very much know they've been in a game

1659 The gaffer is out and about already and is typically proud of how close his team ran City

This Is The Best Trip...

1703   Ian Evatt gives a player's perspective and feels 'gutted' to be taking no points away and that it was ' an awesome experience' playing against Tevez.

1720   Interviews filed, pick up stray son and we're on the way home, both agreeing the result was just about right but also on how well Blackpool played. Traffic is moving and we're home by 1825 ... just in time to make our 1900 rendezvous in the pub!

Manchester City 1 Blackpool 0
(Johnson) -

Manchester City: (4-4-2) Hart; Boateng, Lescott, Kompany, Kolarov; (Zabaleta, 58), De Jong, Barry, Ya Ya Toure, A Johnson: Tevez, Silva (Milner, 63)

Referee: Mark Clattenberg
Attendance: 47,296

Blackpool: (4-3-3) Kingson; Eardley, Evatt, Cathcart, Crainey; Adam, Vaughan, Sylvestre (Phillips, 45); Taylor-Fletcher (Ormerod, 73), Campbell, Varney (Carney, 83)

Miles Travelled: 90
Total Miles: 3,770

Game 20

Birmingham City

Bloomfield Road, 04-01-11

At last - a home game which can go ahead. It's a midweek night match and coincides with my first day back at work but I've no meetings scheduled and am able to get back home for a bowl of soup before departing at 1720. Gary is presenting from the ground and needs me to be there to set up by 1830, which I manage quite comfortably. I nip into Matt's office to drop off a bottle and a belated Christmas card and tonight's team is up on his computer screen.

It will be the one which finished at City so it's one change ... Matt Phillips starts in place of Ludovic Sylvestre. On the way out I bump into Charlie who asks how my day trip to Ibrox went. He'd watched the game on TV and we share views on just how poor Rangers were on the day. Despite that I tell him that the atmosphere was something like I've never witnessed before and he recalls walking out for his first taste of Old Firm fever...' I could nae stop my knees from knocking'...and I could well believe him! On the other side of the ground Gary opens the show at 1900. After giving listeners news of the teams a few minutes later, he asks me to interview some fans and a group near the commentary point oblige. They are all extremely confident that Pool will stay up and each of them predict a home win tonight. Hmmm ... I'm not so sure despite Birmingham's poor away record and that they haven't won at the seaside in eleven attempts stretching back to 1960. Summariser Micky Mellon joins in the pre-match banter and I'm able to tell him about my New Year trip to Ibrox. Micky's persuasion is for the green half of Glasgow so he's more than happy to discuss it ... what a fantastic occasion! All of a sudden it's 2000 and referee Jon Moss signals the beginning of procedings.

2001   Matt Derbyshire has an air shot in front of an open goal - a huge let off!

2004   This time its Cameron Jerome fluffing a close range sitter with Pool all over the place.

2013   Charlie's perfect cross from the left is cracked goal bound by Phillips only to see Ben Foster save with his legs.

2017   Alexander Hleb should have punished an error from Craig Cathcart but can't find the target

2024   Stephen Crainey, mister reliable, uncharacteristically presents Hleb with a gift just inside the box and the Russian squeezes the opener past Richard Kingson
....0-1

2026   Matt Phillips only needs to make contact with a left wing cross but it brushes his forehead and goes wide

2044 Birmingham attack and have a three against two situation but Kingson thwarts Jerome to leave City ahead by a single goal at half-time

2054 Foster saves well from Charlie and Luke Varney can only put the rebound over the top.

2102 The Birmingham keeper denies DJ from close range

2107 Jerome is clear and beats Kingson but the ball comes back off the post. Is this a turning point?

2109 Neal Eardley's neat cross from the right is expertly headed across the box by GTF and DJ volleys the equalizer into the bottom corner 1-1

2112 A double change sees Brett and Jason Euell on for Phillips and GTF and it is Brett who brings another fine save out of Foster

2114 A searing drive from Charlie at last beats the outstanding keeper ... but this one crashes back into play off the far post

2126 Here comes the sickener ... Birmingham sub Beausejour crosses from the right. Roger Johnson knocks it down and centre back partner Scott Dann is all alone to drive past Kingson 1-2

2131 Birmingham deny Pool any possession in stoppage time and seal their first away Premier League win of the season - and a potentially damaging double over Blackpool

2150   The gaffer, who had given fourth official Howard
        Webb real grief about the winner thinking it to be
        offside, comes out of the home dressing room and
        heads straight for the referee's room although the 45
        minute 'cooling off' period is nowhere near up.
        Steve Canavan and I, preparing for the interviews in
        Matt's office fear another long wait. Not so. Ollie is
        allowed entry to see the officials and returns within
        a couple of minutes to begin with the media. It later
        transpires that he's been able to look at the replay
        which does show two City players offside for the
        winning goal when the cross is delivered. Critically,
        however, the two involved in the goal were not
        offside and that's why Mr. Holloway went to see the
        officials ... to tell them they were right and he was
        wrong and tendered an apology which was
        accepted. How common sense ... how refreshing!

2155   Charlie appears for interview and is disappointed
        but not too down stressing the positives from the
        now completed first half of the season. He also
        stresses that he doesn't want to talk about the
        possibility of him moving in the transfer window -
        he 'just wants to play'

2202   Matt brings Ollie into the interview room and as
        usual I switch my machine on. Before I can pose the
        first question, Ollie rips into my 'rascal of a shirt
        Chissie' and it's caught on tape. The studio will
        really go to town with that! The gaffer is also
        disappointed and admits too many of his players
        had an off night. 'Don't congratulate us on having
        25 points ... we need 40 or more and we're nowhere
        near that yet'.

Above: Marlon Harewood fires Blackpool's second goal at Wigan

Left: The Gaffer, Ian Holloway

Below: Harewood and Elliot Grandin celebrate the perfect start in the Premier League

Above: Tough times at Stamford Bridge, but still there were smiles from the Tangerine Army

Right: Scoreboard at Anfield... Ollie's finest hour

Charlie Adam scores from the spot at Newcastle in September

Above: If only dad could have seen me now! The man himself savours the moment

Below: Gary Taylor Fletcher salutes the ecstatic supporters at Anfield

Above: Harewood in scoring action amidst the controversy at Villa

Right: Prince William at Bloomfield...
is he reading my column?

Below: Double delight for DJ at the Stadium of Light

Above: THAT moment... Brett goes into the record books against Spurs

Below: The 'History Man' celebrates with big mate Keith Southern

Above: Howard Webb dismisses protests in ruling out Luke Varney's goals at Blackburn
Below: ...but the gaffer clearly didn't agree with him!

Above: Cue penalty mayhem at White Hart Lane as Fletch is felled by Gomes

Below: Charlie after scoring his last goal at Bloomfield...

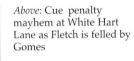

Left: ...and he dedicates it to his adoring fans

Above: It's all over, but Ian Holloway still has the dignity to congratulate Manchester Utd manager Sir Alex Ferguson on his team becoming Champions

Left: It was tense at times - but the Blackpool supporters had a season to remember

2225   Job done and off home to watch The Ashes - and no
beer!

Blackpool 1 Birmingham 2
(Campbell) - (Hleb, Dann)

Blackpool: (4-3-3) Kingson; Eardley, Evatt, Cathcart, Crainey: Adam, Vaughan; Phillips (Ormerod, 70) Taylor-Fletcher (Euell, 70), Campbell, Varney (Southern, 80)

Birmingham: 4-4-2) Foster; Carr, Johnson, Dann, Ridgewell; Hleb (Phillips, 81) Gardner, Ferguson, Fahey (Larsson, 57); Jerome, Derbyshire (Beausejour, 75)

Referee: Jon Moss
Attemdance: 14,550

Miles Travelled: 90
Total Miles: 3,860

97

Game 21

*

Southampton

St Mary's Stadium, FA Cup round three, 08-01-11

This match initally appeared on my schedule but, after a short conversation with Gary and a discussion around BBC finances, a dose of common sense kicked in. So it's Phil Cunliffe who is detailed to the deep south whilst I head north to Deepdale where Billy Davies and Forest are the opposition.

Ian Holloway made it quite clear that he will field a much changed and youthful outfit as the cup is not a priority, so I'm not too upset to be missing a potential 750-mile round trip. After my morning workout I learn that Liverpool have sacked Roy Hodgson and that Kenny Dalglish is to take charge at Anfield until the end of the season. Bollocks! What bad timing ... Liverpool's next league game is the re-arranged affair at the seaside next Wednesday - that's certain to be a much more difficult proposition now.

I arrive at Deepdale to my usual welcome from the car park steward and am all set up by 1315. General Manager Ben Rhodes confirms Phil Brown's first selection as North

End boss and there's no Iain Hume because of a hamstring
… a massive blow. The steak pie and peas are excellent and
I'm back upstairs and ready for the start of the show. Phil
brings the team news from Southampton – only Neal
Eardley and Matt Phillips remain from midweek and there's
a debut in midfield for second year scholar Liam Tomsett as
well as a first start in a year for keeper Paul Rachubka. When
Phil reads the substitutes out, I've only heard of one of the
youngsters, none of the big hitters have even made the
journey. This is going to be a strange afternoon for me. The
radio station is doing split commentaries on both my game
and Blackpool so I won't even get news of how things are
going in my headphones.

1535   Preston's forgotten man Darren Carter curls his side
       ahead from 20 yards.

1546   Half-time arrives at Deepdale and I quickly hand
       over to Phil just as the whistle blows there too. It's
       goalless but listening to his half-time report, Pool's
       youngsters have had to rely on a number of fine
       saves from Chubs to be still in the game.

1605   Paul Anderson races away from the Preston defence
       and finishes well to pull Forest level.

1609   Jon Lowe from the studio tells me that Lee Barnard
       has put Southampton ahead. No surprise really …1-0

1644   More goal news … Guly Do Prado smashes a second
       for Southampton. Ah well, I guess Pool aren't going
       too far in this year's FA Cup 2-0

1645   Forest earn a last-minute corner from which centre

back Luke Chambers pokes home a late winner. It's tough on Preston who certainly didn't deserve to lose

1715   New boss Phil Brown is upbeat and good value in the interview and I wish him well from all at BBC Radio Lancashire

1730   All done and I'm on my way home but it's not until I leave the M6 that I hear Ian Holloway's interview. He's proud of the way his youngsters performed and has special credit for my mate Gary Parkinson's role in their development. Well done gaffer!

Southampton 2 Blackpool 0
(Barnard, Guly) -

Southampton: (4-4-2) Bialkowski; Richardson, Martin, Seaborne, Harding; Lallana, Schneiderlin, Puncheon, Hammond (Dickson, 61); Lambert, Barnard (Oxlade-Camberlain, 84)

Blackpool: (4-3-3) Rachubka; Eardley (Francis-Reynolds, 65), Baptiste, Keinan, Edwards; Southern, Sylvestre, Tomsett (Barkhuizen, 56); Phillips, Euell, Ormerod (Roberts, 76)

Referee: Danny McDermid
Attendance: 21,464

Miles Travelled: 70
Total Miles: 3,930

Game 22

*

Liverpool

Bloomfield Road, 12-01-11

It may be 17 days after schedule but another of the Premier League giants are due in town tonight. Having fired Roy Hodgson at the weekend the messiah, Kenny Dalglish, will be in charge of his beloved Liverpool for the first time in a league game for 20 years.

I can't wait ... but the day starts badly. I've arranged this to be my day off, but overnight rain means no golf as the course is closed. Watching England beat Australia in a T20 cricket match is no real substitute, but nonetheless enjoyable and I combine it with a work out. I then accompany Janis back to work after lunch and have a power walk home and I'm off north nice and early at 1700. All set up by 1815, it's time to go and see Matt and find out how Ian Holloway intends to tackle this one.

There's a buzz in the entrance area as Liverpool arrive - and it's the whole squad, suspended Gerrard and injured Carragher and all. Elliot Grandin, as I anticipated, is back for young Matt Phillips in the only change. Gary and Micky Mellon arrive and with the help of plenty of pre-match audio, it's time for the teams to come out before we know it. There must be in excess of 100 snappers waiting for Kenny who emerges to a blinding flash of whirring shutters. I have to pinch myself to believe I am here at Bloomfield Road commentating when Liverpool are the visitors under the man I used to idolise from the Anfield Kop.

2003   Fernando Torres dances down the right, on into the box, and smashes the opener past Richard Kingson. It could be a long night 0-1

2012   David Vaughan dispossesses Raul Meireles and slides GTF in between Daniel Agger and Martin Skrtel. After a fortunate bounce, GTF coolly rolls the equalizer beyond Pepe Reina. Fletch dashes to the dug out and holds up a shirt - the goal is a tribute to his former team-mate Richard Butcher who died earlier in the week. Super touch 1-1

2017   The goal has knocked Liverpool out of their stride and GTF has a shot parried away by Reina.

2035   Charlie forces a good save from Reina with a fierce left footer

2047   Half-time arrives with and the crowd rises to applaud a terrific half of football.

2112   Reina brilliantly tips Vaughan's effort over the bar

2112   Cross from Milan Jovanovic volleyed over by Torres

2124   Neal Eardley hits a peach of a diagonal cross and Ian Evatt plants a header back across goal. From 12 yards, DJ Campbell guides a header past a wrong footed Reina. Cue, wild tangerine celebration.......2-1

2128 A Charlie Adam thunderbolt just about beaten away by Reina with the Seasiders bossing the game now

2138 Keith Southern and Alex Baptiste enter the fray and provide a midfield shield for what has been an outstanding defence.

2148 Blackpool dominate the latter stages and keep the ball brilliantly throughout four minutes of stoppage time before Michael Oliver signals a league double over mighty Liverpool. The place is bouncing. Who in their right mind would ever have predicted this? The erstwhile Kings of Europe humbled twice by a club which has been forced to live in their shadow for so long. In anybody's book it's an amazing achievement.

2210 I don't think I've ever seen the gaffer so delighted – and that includes at the top of the Wembley steps. Once again my shirt cops some stick – 'You come straight from the golf course Chizzers … on the tee, Ian Chisnall'. Oh no, more joy from the studio boys! Ollie pays tribute to all at the club on how far they have come and, as at Anfield, can't help himself but think about his Dad and his adulation of Liverpool. ' If he could see me now he'd be the proudest bloke on the planet he would!'

2220 Fletch is beaming too and explains the background to his tribute … and is quite emotional in doing so. ' I played with Butch at Lincoln and I only spoke to him last week. I was devastated when I heard the news.' That apart, he's clearly enjoyed his night against his beloved Reds.

2225 There's a terrific spirit in the dressing room corridor as players from both sides chat and swap shirts.DJ emerges from TV interviews and stresses the team ethic and the belief inside that dressing room. 'We can all kick on from here now. We were good value for that...just ask their lads'

2235 Back at the point to file the interviews and Gary is still around talking to Accrington boss, John Coleman in the press box. Eventually, all the stuff is filed and its almost 2300 by the time I'm back in the car. For sure, it's a happy drive home, still rubbing my eyes that 28 points are on the board – and that Blackpool have completed a Premier League double over Liverpool. Never in all my days did I think I'd be able to say that.

Blackpool 2 Liverpool 1
(Taylor-Fletcher, Campbell) - (Torres)

Blackpool: (4-3-3) Kingson; Eardley, Evatt, Cathcart, Crainey; Adam, Vaughan, Grandin (Phillips, 64); Taylor-Fletcher (Baptiste, 83) Campbell,Varney (Southern, 83)

Referee: Michael Oliver
Attendance: 16,089

Liverpool: (4-4-2) Reina; Kelly, Agger, Skrtel, Johnson; Meireles, Lucas, Poulsen (N'Gog, 84); Kuyt (Shelvey, 75) Torres

Miles Travelled: 90
Total Miles: 4,020

Game 23

✴

West Bromwich Albion

The Hawthorns, 15-01-11

T his is a particularly special match day. It's the start of a five day jaunt which will not only take in The Hawthorns but a night in London and four days in Tenerife if all goes well. With the car packed with holiday case, golf clubs and broadcasting kit, Jan and I head off. The motorway is quiet and we're at Hawthorns House by 1220.

Thankfully, it's not raining for the long walk up to the ground and, good club as they are, the Albion people are fine about Janis coming up to the media suite for a coffee before she joins the away fans behind the goal. After a traditional West Midlands balti pie, the Blackpool media staff arrive with reports that Pool are likely to be unchanged. Celebrity Albion fans Frank Skinner and Adrian Chiles appear in the media suite and both are full of praise for the way Blackpool have gone about life in the Premier League. They both wish us well ... but not for the next few hours.

Even by his standards, summariser Steve Canavan is particularly late arriving, but he's safely alongside me on the TV gantry for the kick off at 1500.

1502   DJ Campbell wastes the chance to get Pool off to a flier by dragging his close-range shot wide

1511   West Brom are all over the place as David Vaughan curls a left footer into the net 0-1

1521   Charlie Adam hits the pass of the season to find DJ on the right wing and then surpasses it with a 50-yard volleyed effort on to the chest of Luke Varney

1537   Jerome Thomas is giving Neal Eardley a torrid time and he slips a pass between Blackpool's centre backs for Peter Odemwingie to equalise 1-1

1609   Charlie slides DJ in through the middle and once again the striker pulls it wide when he should be scoring.

1609   How costly that proves as almost immediately yet another Thomas cross is poked home by James Morrison 2-1

1621   Charlie gifts West Brom possession and somehow, Richard Kingson gets him out of jail denying Odemwingie

1627   James Morrison should seal the game but blazes over

1637   Pool sub Matt Phillips curls in a peach of a cross and Gary Taylor Fletcher guides in the leveller.............2-2

1639   Craig Cathcart doesn't deal with a routine long ball and Odemwingie pounces to win it........................3-2

1640   DJ,Brett and GTF all fail to grab a point in a late scramble

1710   The gaffer appears and refuses to blame tiredness or a slightly iffy pitch for the defeat. He is though clearly annoyed that referee Stuart Attwell didn't give an early penalty in DJ's favour

1725   GTF emerges from the tunnel to complete the interviews and says the lads are not too down and were maybe a touch unlucky

1800   Job done and back to the car. But it's the M1 south instead of heading back north with a night in North London ahead before a 0400 drive to Gatwick. A luxury four day break in Tenerife awaits with the opportunity of seeing son Dean and girlfriend Jenna doing a live gig together, and a game of golf on a championship course. Pity the result wasn't right to set us on the way!

West Brom 3 Blackpool 2
(Odemwingie 2, Morrison) - (Vaughan, Taylor-Fletcher)

West Brom: (4-4-2) Myhill; Jara, Tamas, Scharner, Cech; Morrison (Cox, 69) Mulumbu (Shorey, 89) Dorrans (Tchoyi, 84), Brunt; Odemwingie, Thomas

Referee: Stuart Attwell
Attendance: 25,316

Blackpool: (4-3-3) Kingson; Eardley (Ormerod, 66) Cathcart, Evatt, Crainey; Adam,Vaughan, Grandin (Phillips, 53); Taylor-Fletcher, Campbell, Varney (Baptiste, 76)

Miles Travelled: 240
Total Miles: 4,260

Game 24

*

Sunderland

Bloomfield Road, 22-01-11

More matchday anguish...station commentator Andy Bayes is on paternity leave and I've had my trip to Bloomfield Road switched to a less than appetising trip to The Riverside and the North East. Its Middlesbrough and Preston for me but at least I'll have some company. I'm picking up Allan Smart at Junction 29 so I leave a very foggy Newburgh just before 1030.

Passenger collected, we head north catching up on the many events since we last worked together at the end of September. Smartie has some particularly juicy inside knowledge surrounding Big Sam Allardyce's shock departure from Blackburn. It just confirmed my thoughts at the time of just how agents are manipulating the game to suit their own suspect motives. Big Sam was clearly stitched up. The roads are clear and we're parked alongside the Tees at just after 1300. I leave Allan attacking his sweet chilli chicken and enjoy a two-way with Keith Fletcher before eating lunch watching Liverpool win at Wolves - a good result for Pool.

Both Smartie and I see live the Sian Massey incident which was to ultimately cost Richard Keyes and Andy Gray their jobs on SKY...and Ms Massey was bang on correct! The programme is up and running before the first bad news of the day. Gary Hunt brings the team news from Bloomfield ... DJ has been sent home ill, young Matt Phillips will play instead of him. That, in anybody's language, is a huge blow.

1514   This game is struggling to find any rhythm when I'm told to cross to Bloomfield. I can tell by the tone of producer Jon's voice it's not good news. Kieran Richardson has put Sunderland ahead 0-1

1536   Andy Lonergan makes a brilliant double save to keep Preston level just at the moment when I'm advised of a second goal at the seaside...disaster, Richardson has done it again.....................................0-2

1601   More bad news in the headphones - Stephen Crainey has been carried off and with Manchester United due at the seaside on Tuesday, this is turning into a terrible afternoon for Blackpool

1609   Can it get any worse? ... Yes, keeper Richard Kingson is taken off with a head injury

1621   Preston's brave resistance is ended by a 20 yard strike from Boro centre back Matthew Bates

1642   A penalty at Blackpool – and it's a home one converted by Charlie. But it's too late isn't it? 1-2

1644   Billy Jones stoops to head Preston level and North End deserve their point at the death.

This Is The Best Trip...

1647   News that Blackpool have been beaten arrives just as my game ends...1 –2

1715   North End assistant Brian Horton emerges for interview buzzing with what he considered a 'great point'. He also reveals that boss Phil Brown has lost his voice shouting from the touchline.

1720   Goalscorer Billy Jones is good value at interview and already looking forward to a trip to Scunthorpe. How can anybody say that!

1730   All done, nice and early, and as we head out on to the A66, we get the first audio of Ian Holloway on Five Live. He's realistic and says the result is probably a bit of justice after the smash and grab raid at The Stadium of Light

2000   After listening to '606' through the journey, I drop Smartie off in thick fog. We both agree it's not been a great day for a variety of reasons

---

Blackpool 1 Sunderland 2
(Adam, pen) - (Richardson 2)

Blackpool: (4-3-3) Kingson (Rachubka, 56); Eardley, Evatt, Cathcart,Crainey (Ormerod, 49); Adam, Vaughan, Grandin (Harewood, 62); Taylor-Fletcher, Varney, Phillips

Sunderland: (4-4-2) Gordon; Onuoha, Bramble, Ferdinand, Bardsley (Colback, 62); El Mohammady, Hendersron, Zenden, Malbranque (Riveros, 80); Richardson, Gyan

Referee: Lee Mason
Attendance: 16,037

Miles Travelled: 340
Total Miles: 4,600

110

Game 25

*

Manchester United

Bloomfield Road, 25-01-11

With the possible exceptions of Real Madrid and Barcelona, the biggest club in world football is due at Bloomfield Road tonight. Due to the big freeze, the fixture is seven and a half weeks late but what a prospect. I have chosen to have my day off, but again the weather has dictated no chance of golf. So, it's a work out, a late lunch and off to the seaside about 1600 and even as I park up just before 1700, a full two and a half hours prior to kick off, you can feel something special in the air.

I take a trip to the club shop to buy Dean a shirt as a mere token of thanks for the Tenerife trip and there's a buzz all around the outside of the ground. The press room is busy as well and when I make it round to Matt's office, it's no surprise to learn that there won't be a spare seat in the media area. Big Matt is understandably in transfer window stress mode and updates me on the Charlie Adam saga ... we both think this may well be his final game in tangerine. United arrive to much interest in the dressing room area and all the big hitters are here – a real compliment from Sir Alex as to how far Blackpool have come. It's time for the team sheets to go in and Pool have Baps in for the injured Crainey and DJ back from his gastric problem. Berbatov and Rooney are named up top for a full strength United – a chill suddenly does down my spine as I head back to Gary Hickson in the press box. When the Red Devils come out to warm up it's an amazing sight. Fans from all sides flock down to the pitch side and it looks as though everyone has a camera flashing to record the day Manchester United came to Blackpool in the top flight of English football. Andy Morrell joins us, fresh with ten stitches in his forehead...the scars of battle!..and in the midst of an atmosphere I've never felt before at the ground, it's kick-off time.

1935   Charlie falls heavily and needs treatment on his right arm as Blackpool start really well.

1946   The man of the moment has recovered and a 50 yard right foot pass forces Wayne Rooney to concede a corner. Charlie's wicked delivery is powerfully headed home by Craig Cathcart - his first for the club against the team who sold him. Wild joy as the ground erupts and don't Pool deserve it! 1-0

1956   Elliot Grandin blazes a golden chance over the bar

2012   Nemanja Vidic attempts to head a left wing cross behind for a corner but instead Edwin Van Der Sar makes a wonder save to prevent an own goal

2012   Another Charlie corner and another swerving delivery. Its headed on by Nani and DJ squeezes home a second at the back stick. Bloomfield Road is in dreamland...2-0

2017 Half-time and a thunderous standing ovation. Am I fantasizing or have I just seen my team slaughter Manchester United for the whole of the first half? The only problem is that the game should be over ...

2032 Ryan Giggs comes off the bench at the break. Now there's an ominous sign.

2037 Luke Varney is brought down in the penalty area by Rafael ... but Peter Walton refuses the penalty claim. The TV monitors show it's a nailed on spot kick and over in the dugout the whole ground can see the gaffer going absolutely mental. A turning point?

2052 Wayne Rooney gets the hook and Javier Hernanez replaces him

2058 Nani crosses for Dimitar Berbatov to glide in for United. Now it will be the Alamo............................2-1

2101 Chi Chi Hernandez is clean through and beats Richard Kingson to level it up 2-2

2115 It's all United now and Giggs sends Berbatov into the box. Kingson is beaten to his right and United celebrate - with no small relief - in style 2-3

2127 The end of ten minutes of stoppage time accrued for a head injury to Rafael and a shattered Blackpool are devastated in defeat

2145 The gaffer feels like he's 'been kicked in a very painful place' and whilst launching a plea for Charlie to stay until the end of the season, quite rightly felt the result hinged on the penalty call which the referee got wrong. 'Even United wouldn't have come back from three goals down'.

2204   Goalscorer Cathcart gives a view from the dressing room. 'Bitterly disappointed but taking many positives'.

2225   Interviews filed, I'm on my way home. Another magnificent night, but as I drive home I feel drained and as if my team have got nothing from a game in which they have had the best team in the land on the run! 2011 hasn't started well ... we always knew there would be an iffy month in the season. The pity is that it's happened to be January - the month packed with re-arranged fixtures. Suddenly, 40-plus points looks a long way away - as does the six days until the end of the transfer window.

Blackpool 2 Manchester United 3
(Cathcart, Campbell) - (Berbatov2, Hernandez)

Blackpool: (4-3-3) Kingson; Eardley, Cathcart, Evatt, Baptiste: Adam, Vaughan, Grandin; Taylor-Fletcher (Harewood, 73), Campbell, Varney (Phillips, 67)	Man Utd: (4-4-2) VanDer Sar; Rafael (Anderson, 79), Vidic, Smalling, Gibson (Giggs, 45), Scholes, Fletcher, Nani; Berbatov, Rooney (Hernandez. 65)
Referee: Peter Walton Attendance: 15,574	Miles Travelled: 90 Total Miles: 4,690

Monday January 31st

Transfer deadline day has become a real media circus with wall to wall TV coverage. Sky seem to have camera crews everywhere including Squires Gate where various shots are screened of Charlie driving away in a people carrier are shown. Differing reports say he's being driven to Anfield, Old Trafford or all Premier League points in the country ... none of which prove to be true, but then, why let the facts get in the way of a good story?

As the evening goes by, I'm like a cat on a proverbial hot tin roof watching the agony on the TV. At 2230, the ticker on the bottom of the screen claims that Blackpool have rejected bids from Liverpool and Aston Villa for Charlie who will be staying at the club. That does little to calm my agitated state and I'm afraid I have to attack the Bushmills in an effort to settle my nerves. The first sip turns to poison as Sky break a story that Tottenham have had a bid accepted for Adam and it's all about trying to get the paperwork through in time. Midnight at last arrives with no further news ... other than that Spurs have left it too late to complete their move. Phew!!

Oh, by the way, Blackpool have brought in some Premier League experience in James Beattie from Rangers and Andy Reid from Sunderland, both on loan. Jason Puncheon was actually travelling up to Newcastle to sign for his former boss, Alan Pardew, but Ian Holloway's persuasion dragged him to the seaside and an unknown Belarus international centre forward Sergei Kornilenko arrived from Zenit St Petersburg. But still no keeper ... and surprise, surprise, none of the above additions are defenders!

Game 26

*

West Ham United

Bloomfield Road, 02-02-11

With West Brom and Wigan picking up a point each the previous evening, I'm all too aware of the need for Pool to do the same as bottom club West Ham are due in town tonight. The game has been moved back 24 hours because of The Hammers FA Cup tie on Sunday and that switch has caused me some problems. I have to do a presentation to the Governors at school in my 'day' job so I'm hoping they'll re-arrange the agenda and let me go on first. Sure enough, a word to a good friend and chairperson, Sue and I'm all done by 1600 so it's off home for a bowl of soup and to collect the kit.

The motorway is quiet and I'm in Matt's office at 1815 where he gives me a blow by blow account of transfer deadline day and the saga surrounding Charlie. Right on cue and just as he's finishing, in comes Mr Adam, the man at the centre of all the furore. 'I sat in that f...ing chair for seven hours on Monday!' he laughs and gives his own version of the late bid by Tottenham. Charlie and his agent had given up the prospect of a move by about 2230 and left the ground to find something to eat. Just as he had taken his first bite, his agent's phone rang with Spurs on the other end of it. Food abandoned, it was back to Bloomers for another vigil in the chair until the midnight hour had passed. I ask how he feels and he's realistic enough to know that he's got two missions – one to help keep Blackpool up and the other to play his part so he gets his big move in the summer with everybody's blessing. Top man! After he leaves, Matt reveals that the gaffer has made changes – and he's left out big Evo…that's a real stunner! Bap is to play centre back with David Carney coming in and there's a debut for Andy Reid, Elliot Grandin making way.

I drop in at the media office and engage in some banter with Stewart, Alec and Simon Crabtree from Premier League Productions. Suddenly the door opens and in comes an incredulous Ian Evatt. The room falls silent as he tells us he's been left out - he simply can't believe it and says I can put that out on air as well! He leaves clearly furious and still shaking his head and we're like naughty school children just looking at each other. Perhaps it's safer on the other side of the ground, so I'm off to join Andy Morrell for the 2000 start.

2001   Richard Kingson pulls off a smart save to deny Victor Obinna an opening goal

2001   With Blackpool looking decidedly disjointed Kingson does brilliantly to keep out Gary O'Neill's effort.

2022   It's all West Ham and Kingson gets down well to save Craig Cathcart's poor touch

2023   Obinna hits a tame shot to Kingson's near post and this time the keeper shovels it in for a howler.......0-1

This Is The Best Trip...

2035   Pool's first effort sees Robert Green back pedal to palm over Andy Reid's curler

2037   Blackpool make a meal of clearing a cross and Robbie Keane scores on his West Ham debut 0-2

2042   Charlie Adam drives in a low corner from the right and it skids straight in 1-2

2043   Straight from the kick off, Obinna leathers a belter from 20 yards into the top corner..............................1-3

2101   Evatt replaces Craig Cathcart at the break

2117   James Beattie comes on for a Pool debut with Marlon Harewood giving way

2125   Neal Eardley's 25-yard free kick thumps back off the angle of bar and post in what proved to be Blackpool's last clear cut chance

2148   Referee Stuart Attwell brings a miserable evening to a close

2210   A dejected but fair Ian Holloway admits his team were beaten by a better side. He pays credit to Charlie for putting the saga of the last month behind him and hints at changes for the weekend clash at Everton

2220   Newcomer Andy Reid gives his views on his move to the seaside and on his hour long stint on the pitch.

2245   Interviews filed, I head for the car park with an

apprehensive feeling. This was a game from which Pool desperately needed to take something. Instead, they've been well beaten and the gap is narrowing by the minute. It could be a long, long time until May 22nd.

Blackpool 1 West Ham 3
(Adam) - (Obinna 2, Keane)

Blackpool: (4-3-3) Kingson; Eardley, Cathcart (Evatt, 45), Baptiste, Carney, Adam, Vaughan, Reid (Harewood, 60); Taylor-Fletcher, Campbell, Varney (Beattie, 60)

West Ham: (4-4-2) Green; Jacobsen, Tomkins, Gabbidon (Reid, 33), Bridge; O'Neill, Noble, Parker, Obinna (Kovac, 85); Piquionne, Keane (Boa-Morte, 84)

Referee: Stuart Attwell
Attendance: 15,095

Miles travelled: 90
Total Miles: 4,780

Game 27

*

Everton

Goodison Park, 05-02-11

A horribly wet morning means no walk to Parbold for the morning paper and I'm not relishing the prospect of the trek from the car park in Stanley Park to Goodison. If anything, the monsoon is heavier as I leave home at 1145 and it's no real surprise that the East Lancs Road is awash in the usual places.

After the problems accessing Stanley Park for the Liverpool game, I'm relieved to be waved straight through this time. Then, under the biggest golf umbrella I can lay my hands on, it's off on the 15 minute walk to the ground. It must be 25 years since I worked at Everton but, on arrival, it's clear that not much has changed. It must be the most cramped press box in the Premier League, but I'm safely set up with equipment tested by 1300. I lunch with good friends, Gary Flintoff and Steve Roberts, colleagues from BBC Merseyside, and try to ring Matt for team news - to no avail. So it's an anxious wait right up until 1400 to see who Ian Holloway has selected.

Out on the pitch Richard Kingson is going through a

strenuous warm up - surely Paul Rachubka will be preferred today. And so it proves when a copy of the team sheets arrive – Chubs is one of five changes. The others see Evatt start in place of the injured Cathcart and Puncheon and Beattie get first starts with a recall for Elliot Grandin. Kingson, Varney and Reid drop to the bench with Taylor-Fletcher rested. Steve Canavan squeezes himself into place and we're read to rock and roll at 1500 with Phil Cunliffe presenting the show.

1520   Dinyar Bilyaletdinov tortures Neal Eardley and crosses from the bye line for Louis Saha to open the scoring. It's been coming 1-0

1537   Blackpool win a corner from the right and Charlie tries the low drive routine again. Big Evo's cute back heel is over the line before it's hooked out but Alex Baptiste follows up to equalise 1-1

1540   Real controversy as David Carney fouls Seamus Coleman on the left edge of the box. The ball breaks to Saha who sweeps it in ... but referee Kevin Friend has blown too early for the foul and despite a seething Goodison, the 'goal' is disallowed.

1544   The pot is still boiling as Mr Friend blows for half-time. A good name for a man who has none in blue.

1604   Leighton Baines cuts a low ball into the near post and Saha glides it past a helpless Chubs 2-1

1606   The Pool keeper brilliantly denies the Russian Bilyaletdinov from point-blank range as Everton swarm all over the Seasiders.

1619 Incredibly, Pool draw level. James Beattie does well to cross from the left but it's behind DJ. New boy Jason Puncheon though picks his spot between defenders and it's all square 2-2

1621 Seaside supporters drift into dreamland as DJ's effort comes back off the bar for Charlie to head home the rebound...2-3

1622 Chubs comes out of his area and tries to dribble round Marouanne Fellaini. The Belgian nicks possession and chips goal bound only to see a retreating Ian Evatt pull off one of the most heroic goal-line clearances I've ever seen.

1631 Ian Holloway sends on Rob Edwards and Keith Southern in an attempt to shore up the lead.

1632 Before either substitute has touched the ball and with Charlie off the pitch having treatment, Louis Saha heads his hat-trick goal from Mikel Arteta's corner 3-3

1636 Everton sub Jermaine Beckford beats Baptiste and volleys the home side ahead 4-3

1640 With Blackpool over committed up the pitch Saha makes it a four goal haul and the game is over.....5-3

1720 A shell-shocked gaffer appears for interview and slaughters me for a poor first question as I begin with 'Well Ian, it's another defeat'. 'Nice to see you've been watching the game Chissie - can we have a decent question now?' He's tetchy and upset

- but 100 per cent correct. It was a shocking way to begin an interview with a losing manager. He then concedes that his substitutions didn't get the chance to alter the flow of the game. 'Maybe I should have brought in four defenders in the window'. He adds that the players are 'really low'.

1730   Ian Evatt proves the point. The usually chirpy defender is a downcast man as he bemoans the third Everton goal in particular. It's that ridiculous rule regarding a player having to leave the pitch after treatment that has cost Blackpool … AGAIN!

1750   It's time for that trusted umbrella again as the incessant rain continues to pour down. By the time I reach the car I'm soaked to the skin, probably more by sweat than the rain. To cap off a bad day for Pool results wise, Radio Five Live tell me that Wolves are beating Manchester United. I'm so pissed off, I can't even be bothered going to the pub!

Everton 5 Blackpool 3
(Saha 4, Beckford) - (Baptiste, Puncheon, Adam)

Everton: (4-4-2) Howard; Neville, Distin, Heitinga, Baines; Bilyaletdinov (Beckford, 69) Rodwell (Cahill, 69) Arteta, Fellaini, Coleman: Saha (Jagielka, 85)

Blackpool: (4-3-3) Rachubka; Eardley, Evatt, Baptiste, Carney; Adam, Vaughan, Grandin; Beattie (Harewood, 80), Campbell (Southern, 74), Puncheon (Edwards, 74)

Referee: Kevin Friend
Attendance: 38,202

Miles Travelled: 60
Total Miles: 4,840

Game 28

*

Aston Villa

Bloomfield Road, 16-02-11

I'll have company today ... Dean and Jenna have travelled north for a few days. Yesterday saw a soggy game of golf and a splendid meal at The High Moor, but at least for Dean and myself, this game is the centre point of the weekend. With him leaving the decision to come until late, Dean's had to talk extremely nicely to Matt Williams, but good lad that he is, he sorts a couple of tickets ... and Jenna genuinely looks excited!

Off we go at 1145 and just about an hour later we're safely installed in the car park with the last surviving bricks and mortar of the once famous Mecca Ballroom. My guests are off for a walk along the prom - a real education for a Glasgow girl - and I'm off to set up. All tests done and it's round to the tunnel to see who the gaffer has selected in an attempt to stop the rot. "Reg" Varney pops into the media office just before 1330 but says that the team hasn't been announced yet. Five minutes later, after a flurry of activity in the dressing room corridor, I'm off to Matt's office for the inside info. Pool make four changes - Richard Kingson back in goal for the injury blighted Paul Rachubka, Neal Eardley dropping to the bench to accommodate a fit again Craig Cathcart, Varney preferred to Jason Puncheon and the real surprise is a start for Marlon Harewood with James Beattie on the bench. Second guess Mr Holloway … don't even think of it! Back on the other side, the show opens at 1400 with the concentration on our two commentary games involving Preston and Burnley. But we get to 1500 and in brilliant sunshine, a huge match is off bang on the dot.

1510   With tangerine shirts pouring forward, Brad Friedel takes Baptiste's cross and bowls it out to Darren Bent. An £18 million flick has Gabby Agbonlahor racing 50 yards to round Kingson and slide home from a narrow angle 0-1

1514   Elliot Grandin glances a near post header into the back of the net on the end of Charlie's superb corner for his first goal for Blackpool....................................1-1

1516   An inviting Harewood cross is headed wastefully wide by Varney

1516   Kingson saves with his legs as Stewart Downing is through

1531   The same Villa man curls a shot against a post

1544   Kingson brilliant again, this time to deny Cameroon midfielder Makoun

1537   Scorer Grandin goes off with a tight hamstring - Jason Puncheon is his replacement

This Is The Best Trip...

1544   Half-time comes - how are Blackpool still in this game?

1606   Luke Varney blazes over when well placed

1611   Varney crosses but DJ can only steer it wide - but this is much better from Pool

1623   Marlon Harewood lifts a shot over the bar and is immediately replaced by Matt Phillips

1625   Puncheon fires what proves to be Blackpool's best chance of the half wide

1629   Villa are struggling and Jean Makoun lunges wildly at DJ...Howard Webb whips out the red card and he's off. Ten man Villa try to shut up shop.

1649   A stoppage time break from Ashley Young has about 15,000 hearts in mouths but he pulls his effort badly wide. It's over and it's such a welcome point.

1710   Ian Holloway is bright and before expressing his relief, hammers Steve Canavan's new haircut. The gaffer is happy with the point and goes on to explain the situation with regard to finding another goalkeeper. 'We've enquired after a couple but one didn't want to come and we were a million miles from affording the other!'

1720   Elliot Grandin gives his first ever interview and it's a test for his English more than my French. But he's good value and with some compromises on both sides we get there in the end.

1743   All done and I meet Dean and Jenna outside.
       They've both enjoyed what was a terrific game of
       football - yes, even Jenna who has bought herself a
       Blackpool shirt. Another convert!

Blackpool 1 Aston Villa 1
(Grandin) - (Agbonlahor)

Blackpool: (4-3-3) Kingson; Baptiste, Evatt, Cathcart, Carney; Adam, Vaughan, Grandin (Puncheon, 38); Varney (Reid, 71), Harewood (Phillips, 68), Campbell

Aston Villa: (4-4-2) Friedel; Walker, Cuellar (Collins, 27), Dunne, Clark; Agbonlahor (Bradley, 72), Reo-Coker, Makoun, Downing; Bent (Heskey, 56), Young

Referee: Howard Webb
Attendance: 16,000

Miles Travelled: 90
Total Miles: 4,930

Game 29

*

Tottenham Hotspur
Bloomfield Road, 22-02-11

There's a house full of visitors all booked in for this vital game. Dean and Jenna have come straight off a flight from their gig in Tenerife and, rather less glamourously, sister-in-law Helen and family have driven over after staying in Chesterfield with son Adam already clad in tangerine. After paddling round an extremely sodden golf course, its lunch and an early dart to the seaside … I'm determined to carry out my superstitious walk along the prom to the South Pier. It's a long story but the bottom line is that Pool usually do well if I've had my constitutional!

Walk completed, I'm back to the ground to set up and check the equipment before going to see the boys in the media office. Banter is top quality and I'm drawn to comment that I hope the team are in as good a vein of form from kick off time! I disturb Matt in the middle of his tea, but I'm not the only one. Evo and Charlie are in as well because there are evidently problems with tickets, but after they depart I find that there are to be four changes tonight. Alex Baptiste switches to left back with Neal Eardley recalled;

Ludovic Sylvestre replaces injured compatriot Elliot Grandin, James Beattie is preferred to Luke Varney and here's the big shock - untried, unfit Russian Sergei Kornilenko is thrown in for Marlon Harewood. In anybody's books, that has to be a major gamble even by Mr Holloway's standards.

Over at the press box, summariser Micky Mellon and presenter Gary Hickson are just getting installed for a 1900 start to the programme. Between then and kick off time, I'm dispatched to interview BBC London summariser Bradley Allen - what a nice guy! Astutely, he says that well as Spurs have been playing, they are still brittle at the back and will always give the opposition a chance. We'll see.

2001   First touch for Kornilenko - he's a physical unit alright!

2018   Spurs centre back Sebastian Bassong clumsily hauls down DJ and Chris Foy points to the spot. Charlie goes to the right of Heurelho Gomes and into the corner 1-0

2033   Jermaine Defoe's goal-bound effort is headed from underneath the angle of bar and post by Craig Cathcart... brilliant defending by the Irishman.

2044   Alex Baptiste clears off the line from Roman Pavlyuchenko and Pool break swiftly..up the left. DJ sends Kornilenko goalwards and his cute back heel enables James Beattie to measure a cross. DJ cracks it home from ten yards for a huge half-time lead 2-0

2104   Steven Pienaar fires high and wide after cutting in from the left.

This Is The Best Trip...

2108 Richard Kingson, who had resembled an absolute novice in the first half, saves brilliantly to deny Pavlyuchenko from point blank range.

2110 Luca Modric blazes over after some brilliant Spurs passing.

2116 Blackpool can't stem the white tide and its no surprise to see Keith Southern replace Sylvestre

2119 Spurs have changed things too and substitute Nico Kranjcar shoots over the bar.

2128 Kingson finds a double save and once again Pavlyuchenko can't believe he hasn't scored.

2130 With Brett and Matt Phillips also on now, Baptiste comes up with another goal line clearance.

2139 Stand by for Bloomfield Road to erupt...Phillips cuts into the box and Assou-Ekoto's attempted clearance falls for Brett to drive home. It's the history making goal that he has been chasing since day one at Wigan. In sealing a famous win, Brett has become the first man in history to score for Blackpool in all four divisions. The ground goes mental 3-0

2150 Charlie is feeling his left hamstring and is a virtual passenger. The bench try to get him off but he ignores them and sets off with the ball through the middle. He overruns it and lunges into Michael Dawson to see referee Foy brandishing the yellow card that means a two match ban. Wolves boss Mick McCarthy, watching from the main stand, was later to say that the booking was to change the course of the whole season for Pool and Wolves.

2153   Pavlyuchenko's late volley deflects off the excellent Cathcart and beats Kingson with the last kick of the match..3-1

2210   Matt brings a beaming gaffer into the interview room where he eulogises about the spirit in the camp, typified by the likes of Brett 'words can't describe how proud I am! Just look at the likes of Fletch and Brett. They've dragged themselves out of non league and did they look out of place out there with the best Chizzers? They're a total credit to themselves, their families and this football club'.

2220   I interview the 'history man' who in typical Ormerod fashion, plays down his unique achievement. Whilst many, including myself, have been worried that after those glaring misses on the first day at Wigan, he might not get his place in the club's folk-lore, Brett just shrugged and said the points were more important. At the end of the interview I get a huge hug from a man who has never forgotten that day at Wycombe all those years ago when he had his leg broken. I went to see him in the dressing room at half-time and he asked me to let his mum and dad know in my second half commentary that he was OK. I was happy to oblige then - and even more happy for him now.

2238   Interviews filed, I just about float back to the car on a mixture of adrenalin and emotion. An incredible night!

Blackpool 3 Spurs 1

(Adam, pen. Campbell, Ormerod) - (Pavlyuchenko)

Blackpool: (4-3-3) Kingson; Eardley, Evatt, Cathcart, Baptiste; Adam, Vaughan, Sylvestre (Southern, 58); Beattie (Phillips, 62) Kornilenko (Ormerod, 62) Campbell

Referee: Chris Foy
Attendance: 16,069

Spurs: (4-4-2) Gomes; Gallas, Bassong (Crouch, 73) Dawson, Assou-Ekoto; Lennon, Palacios (Jenas, 45) Modric, Pienaar; Pavlyuchenko, Defoe

Miles Travelled: 90
Total Miles: 5,020

Game 30

*

Wolverhampton Wanderers

Molineux, 26-02-11

Even as long ago as last June when the fixtures were published, this was always going to be a crunch relegation six pointer and so it proves. A massive game it has become now with a suspended Mr Adam … and he's not the only one missing it. Andy Bayes is heading for the West Midlands with me off to Deepdale for the big Lancashire 'derby' with Burnley. He'd rather be where I'll be and I'd definitely sooner be at Wolves … but neither Andy or myself make those crucial decisions, so we'll just have to get on with it.

The morning is distinctly damp, so no walk to the paper shop for me and I spend the morning recovering from a sportsman's dinner the night before. BBC North West are doing a special feature from Deepdale and they've asked my summariser David Eyres and myself to be at the ground early. Sure enough, we're filmed and interviewed around 1300 whilst I set up the equipment. Then it's off for pie and peas to be back in place for Phil Cunliffe to open the show at 1400. Team news is in from Molineux by 1410…Charlie's replacement is to be Keith Southern in the only change. Bayesy can also report Marlon Harewood has gone out on loan to Barnsley with the official club line being that he needs games. I'm not entirely surprised or indeed ready to believe that ... a major training ground bust up with the gaffer has been the big rumour of late. Back here at Deepdale, the atmosphere builds and Howard Webb signals the start of the 136th meeting between these clubs at 1500.

1502   An afternoon of misery doesn't take long to start unfolding...Jon Lowe gives me an early goal from the Premier League, Matt Jarvis has given Wolves the lead 1-0

1523   Paul Coutts sends Barry Nicholson into the box and in the act of falling he manages to lift the ball over Lee Grant to give Preston the lead.

1531   Burnley draw level as Jay Rodriguez' smart finish to a delightful Chris Eagles pass beats Iain Turner.

1538   News of a straight red card at Wolves...DJ off for violent conduct. That carries an automatic three match ban. Disaster!

1546   Half-time both here and at Molineux. Andy Bayes reports Blackpool to be struggling in every department.

1610   Pool's ten men concede another - Jamie O'Hara makes it 2-0. This could be a case of how many?..2-0

1614   Chris Eagles goes down in the box but referee Webb is unimpressed.

1628   Sean St Ledger's weak back header presents Eagles a golden chance but he can only lob tamely into Turner's arms.

1634   Wolves sub Sylvain Ebanks-Blake wraps up the points at Molyneux..3-0

1644   Wade Elliott's superb cross is headed home by Jack Cork and Burnley have a derby victory.

1652   Just as the final whistle sounds at Deepdale, Ebanks-Blake puts the final nail in Blackpool's sorry coffin 4-0

1700   TV film my reaction to the Lancashire derby result pitchside as I wait for both managers.

1710   No surprise to see that it's Eddie Howe first. He's a man of few words but I manage to squeeze about three minutes out of him.

1720   Howe is on his way back across the pitch as Ben Rhodes brings a clearly unhappy Phil Brown the other way. No hand-shake, no words, not even a glance as the managers pass each other. I could be in for a rough ride here...but, fair play to Brownie, after a volley of un-broadcastable invective, he gives an honest account of his situation.

1725   Jack Cork presents the typical picture of a derby match winner to conclude my pitchside interviews.

1750   All clips safely received by studio and I'm on my way home. I don't hear anything of Ian Holloway

until I'm going down Parbold Hill at 1805. He's glad
he hasn't had to 'stomach many days like this one'
and rightly condemns DJ's actions as 'unacceptable.'
As he finishes with the predictable 'we'll have to get
on with it without Mr Adam and Mr Campbell
against Chelsea.' I can't help wondering whether
Saturday February 26th was a day of damaging self-
destruction. The goal difference column has taken a
crucial hammering too.

Wolves 4 Blackpool 0
(Jarvis, O'Hara, Ebanks-Blake 2) -

Wolves: (4-5-1) Hennessey; Zubar (Ebanks-Blake, 55) Stearman, Berra, Elokobi; Jarvis, Edwards (Ward, 65), Henry, O'Hara, Hammil (Foley, 36); Doyle

Referee: Neil Swarbrick
Attendance: 29,086

Blackpool: (4-3-3) Kingson; Eardley, Evatt, Cathcart, Baptiste; Sylvestre (Ormerod, 61), Vaughan, Southern; Kornilenko (Varney, 29), Beattie (Phillips, 61), Campbell

Miles Travelled: 70
Total Miles: 5,090

Game 31

Chelsea

Bloomfield Road, 07-03-11

This will be by far and away my most unusual match day of the season so far. I normally wake up 35 miles from Bloomfield Road on a home match day. Today, I wake less than 35 miles from Stamford Bridge! Jan's birthday weekend has seen us at Craig and Rachel's in Sawbridgeworth since Thursday. Since then, I've crammed the car with wine on a day trip to France (and no, I haven't drunk all of the last lot yet!) and covered Leyton Orient v Notts.County before enjoying a family meal at the local Mexican.

We set off back to the north west at 0930 and just about four trouble free hours later, we're back home in Newburgh. The car sighs with relief as 45 cases of wine are unloaded and I even manage to mow the lawns before leaving for the seaside. This is for sure the biggest test yet bearing in mind that Charlie and DJ will miss the visit of the in-form champions through suspension and I can't help but speculate about the gaffer's team selection. Again, the roads are clear and it's the usual routine on arrival at the ground.

Tests conducted, it's straight to the media office for news of who is going to be asked to plug the huge gaps in the line up. Yet again, nobody can second guess Mr Holloway and there'll be four changes from the side mauled at Wolves: Jason Puncheon replaces DJ and Sylvestre makes way for Andy Reid. Craig Cathcart has developed a mystery virus and Stephen Crainey returns with 'Bap' reverting to centre back. David Carney comes in for Sergei Kornilenko in what will be an unusual 4-3-2-1 formation with James Beattie the lone ranger up top. It looks like an exercise to try and contain Chelsea - a tactic that was adopted in September at Stamford Bridge: a tactic that saw Pool behind inside a minute and four down by half-time ... and a tactic that was abandoned at half-time and apologised for by the manager. I've got one of those cold shivers down my backbone as I head back to the press box to join Gazza and Andy Morrell. Amidst an atmosphere that's building by the minute, it's 2000 and kick-off time before we know it.

2009   Richard Kingson needs extensive treatment after a collision with Didier Drogba

2019   A classic commentary moment: Blackpool concede a cheap corner and I say 'we all know how dangerous Chelsea can be from these situations.' Oops!

2020   Frank Lampard swings in the corner, James Beattie loses his man and John Terry has a free .header from six yards to open the scoring 0-1

2023   Kingson claws away a curler from Jose Bosingwa

2033   Jason Puncheon's 20-yard left footer is shovelled on to the post by Petr Cech

2035 David Carney's goalbound shot is blocked by David Luiz

2036 In Blackpool's best spell of the game, Cech palms away Ian Evatt's cross cum shot for a corner and Chelsea will have a narrow lead at the break.

2111 Solomon Kalou replaces a limping Drogba and at once Chelsea look more lively

2116 Kingson signals to the bench that he wants to come off and Mark Halstead prepares to make his Premier League debut.

2117 Kalou goes down in the box under Evatt's challenge and Mike Dean can't wait to point to the spot. Evatt is distraught and the replays show it's a harsh award. The TV shots of the bench indicate that the gaffer clearly doesn't agree with it

2119 Lampard scores with ease from the spot 0-2

2122 With the goalkeeping change still not made Lampard strolls unchallenged into the box and fires a third low past Kingson. The substitution is made and I fear for young Mark and his shellshocked team mates 0-3

2137 Substitute Matt Phillips is sent clear by Beattie but pulls his shot wide. What a chance!

2141 Beattie releases Jason Puncheon and he shows Phillips how to beat Cech to his left for a smart goal 1-3

2144   Another from the bench, Brett Ormerod, has his
        close range effort diverted behind by Terry. Crazily,
        it could even have been all square

2202   You don't have to be a rocket scientist to gather that
        Mr Holloway is far from happy. He and video
        analyst Liam appear briefly and then disappear into
        his office. The gaffer wants to see the DVD of the
        penalty decision before TV and press interviews

2205   Young Mark Halstead shows for interview and he's
        delighted with his cameo 25 minutes. He's good
        value at the other end of a microphone too.

2215   Matt brings Ian Holloway in and before the
        machines are switched on, he gives a candid opinion
        on referee Dean. He then reverts to interview mode
        and reassures everyone that 'nobody at this club will
        down tools until the very end'. For just about the
        first time, I sense a little unease about the gaffer.

Blackpool 1 Chelsea 3
(Puncheon) - (Terry, Lampard 2, 1 pen)

Blackpool: (4-3-2-1) Kingson (Halstead, 66); Eardley, Evatt, Baptiste, Crainey; Southern, Vaughan, Carney (Ormerod, 73); Puncheon, Reid (Phillips, 73); Beattie

Chelsea: (4-4-2) Cech; Bosingwa, Terry, Luiz, Cole; Essien, Lampard, Ramires (McEachran, 73), Zhirkov (Malouda, 71); Torres, Drogba (Kalou, 54)

Referee: Mike Dean
Attendance: 15,584

Miles Travelled: 90
Total Miles: 5,180

Game 32

*

Blackburn Rovers

Ewood Road, 19-03-11

The Premier League table tells us that this is a huge game for both teams and it seems ages since the Chelsea defeat. There has been bad news in the interim though ... First choice keeper Matt Gilks had targeted this game for his comeback, but he had to limp out of a reserve game after just 14 minutes so it will be Richard Kingson again in goal. It's an early morning work out for me as I catch up with the previous night's Super League rugby on the TV.

I'm really looking forward to the afternoon ahead which is going to be a mega-production from BBC Radio Lancashire. Andy Bayes is presenting the show live from the ground and I will have two top summarisers - Kevin Gallagher from the Rovers angle and Paul Simpson, a promotion winner in tangerine. I leave early as I need to call in at the golf club and, whilst there, I get the anticipated stick from a couple of Rovers fans. But I give as good as I get and I'm on my way in a matter of minutes. It's an absolutely perfect day as I arrive in the car park - at exactly the same time as Bayesy, so we walk across to the ground together. Equipment set up and checked, its lunch time and we share a table with Ian Bryson, another regular contributor to BBC Lancashire's sports output, and Five Live's Alistair Bruce-Ball. Traditional Lancashire hot pot is appropriate fayre for a derby encounter and with ever such a slight anxiety that neither summariser has appeared by 1345, two o'clock looms closer. As Bayesy opens the show, I ring Matt for the Pool team news ... five changes! Charlie is back from suspension, Craig Cathcart is over his illness, Elliot Grandin is fit again and it's a return for tried and trusted GTF and Reg Varney. All in all, it's a typically attack minded starting eleven and with Simmo and Kevin Gallagher safely installed, the time to kick-off just disappears.

1521   Charlie takes a free-kick and 'Reg' Varney reacts first to guide it past Paul Robinson. 5,000 Blackpool fans in the Darwen End go crazy... but the cheers choke in their throats. Howard Webb looked happy enough with the goal but his linesman, Mr Garrett, had raised the flag. No goal the decision - and already we've seen the replays. Correct.

1525   Jason Puncheon rolls in GTF down the right but his shot is high and wide. Ryan Nelsen had challenged Fletch in the act of shooting and referee Webb is the only one in the ground who thinks it's a penalty and a bemused hush follows when he points to the spot. Charlie sends Robinson the wrong way...................0-1

1529   Blackburn are still seething and give away a free kick 28 yards out. Blackpool form a mini wall in front of the Rovers assembly and Charlie finds the 'postage stamp' with a magnificent strike..............0-2

1540 Charlie's shot comes back off Paul Robinson and once again Varney finds the back of the net. Same end, same linesman, same flag, same outcome and again, same correct offside judgement.

1546 Half-time and it brings completely opposite reactions from either end of the ground. Pool get a standing ovation whilst the home side are resoundingly booed off.

1604 Junior Hoilett continues to give Bap an uncomfortable afternoon and his cut back is blazed into the side netting by Steven Nzonzi - who knows he should have scored. It's definitely a case of warning signs flashing

1607 But they go unheeded! Blackpool have chances to clear but can't manage it and skipper Chris Samba drills home from 12 yards...1-2

1648 With Phil Jones, Pederson and Jason Roberts all on by now, Blackburn are reverting to type and bombarding the Blackpool goal with a selection of long throws and free kicks.

1648 Blackpool have somehow survived the 90 minutes, but an extra four minutes are signalled.

1651 GTF is clearly fouled on the Blackburn bye line and is outraged when referee Webb simply points for a goal kick.

1652 Blackburn win a free kick half way inside their own half which Paul Robinson fires high, long and straight. Richard Kingson, for reasons known only to himself, comes into a ruck of players, flaps and Hoilett heads into an empty net. Gut wrenching ..2-2

1653 It's all over and whilst I suspect Pool would have taken a point at kick off, it definitely feels like a defeat now.

1718 Charlie shows for interview and is convinced that GTF was fouled right at the death. Typically he plays down his wonder free kick and is pretty convincing when he says they'll be OK.

1722 Matt has Ollie waiting pitch side and the gaffer says he's a very happy man largely on the quality of his side's performance. He is though - and quite rightly on the day - critical of Howard Webb but with some balance. Yes, he's angry at the injustice done to Fletch at the end and yes, he feels that if a free-kick had been awarded, his team would have seen the game out and taken all three points. But he does also make the point that Mr Webb was the only one in the ground who saw enough to award the penalty. Ollie also says he's off to Spain in the international break to watch the national team and the U19s train.

1735 I'm on my way back to the press box when I learn that Steve Kean has just gone into the media theatre. I interview him after he's done the written boys and he's delighted with the spirit his team showed in coming back. I'll bet he is!

1750 Back upstairs, Simmo and Kev have stayed with Bayesy for a special phone in. It's a great idea...but it means I'll have to hang around until the show goes off air at 1830 as they're using my kit. No pub for me tonight then!

Blackburn 2 Blackpool 2
(Samba, Hoilett) - (Adam 2, 1 pen)

Blackburn Rovers: (4-4-2) Robinson; Salgado, Samba, Nelsen, Olsson: Emerton (P Jones, 58), J. Jones, Nzonzi (Roberts, 71) Hoilett; Santa Cruz, Biram Diouf (Pederson, 71)

Blackpool: (4-3-3) Kingson; Baptiste, Evatt, Cathcart, Crainey; Adam (Southern, 80) Vaughan, Grandin (Phillips, 65) Taylor-Fletcher, Varney (Reid, 80) Puncheon

Referee: Howard Webb
Attendance: 27,209

Miles Travelled: 90
Total Miles: 5,270

145

Game 33

*

Fulham

Craven Cottage, 03-04-11

Matchday preparations begin on the Saturday evening ahead of the Sunday lunchtime kick off for TV ... approximately 1,000 miles from West London! It's the spring break for schools so I'm in Spain at Nerja on the Costa del Sol at a familiar haunt, hence I'm more than confident of finding a bar which will televise the game. But just to make doubly sure, I stroll up the hill from our apartment to The Sportsman's Bar where I watch the first half of Arsenal – Blackburn in the late TV game. Chatting to the owner, Andy Dixon, I learn that he used to play professionally for Grimsby Town and he's well impressed by my knowledge of some of his former team mates and managers, and yes, the Pool game will definitely be on tomorrow.

Sunday dawns and the weather men have got it right. After three days of brilliant sunshine, the crucial yellow object is missing from the sky and it looks likely to be for the duration. So it's a brisk walk around the resort after breakfast before a spot of light lunch and Jan and I are in pole position at 1425 Central European Time. I can't believe the team when the pictures flash up on screen … James Beattie and Brett Ormerod will join GTF up front with Richard Kingson continuing in goal. Ah well, the gaffer knows best … I hope! Sure enough, Blackpool start well and move the ball nicely …

1453 (CET) James Beattie's attempt to find Charlie on half way only sets Bobby Zamora charging goalwards. Zamora resists half hearted challenges to hammer home past Kingson 1-0

1458 Stephen Crainey is harshly penalised in the corner as Damien Duff goes down. Duff strolls into the box, and he and Zamora have a conversation. Duff then proceeds to deliver the free kick to the near post where Zamora comes off Craig Cathcart and the flick header flies in...2-0

These events are being greeted with silence in this particular corner of Spain!

1512 Brett heads Cathcart's long straight ball over keeper Schwarzer but defender Chris Baird clears comfortably off the line.

1519 Half-time and Blackpool's body language isn't great as they trudge off. Time for another pint in Spain.

1551 Beattie clips the outside of a post but Schwarzer had it covered.

1601 Game set and match. The excellent Danny Murphy's free kick is headed against the post by Clint

Dempsey and when it comes back across goal, Dickson Etuhu taps home the clincher. 3-0

1616   GTF shoots wide when well placed to sum up a miserable afternoon for Pool who, without doubt, got exactly what they deserved.

1639   Referee Stuart Attwell signals the end and Jan and I pay the bar bill and depart the scene fearing the worst. I do, however, promise not to let the disaster spoil the holiday.

Fulham 3 Blackpool 0
(Zamora 2, Etuhu) -

Fulham: (4-4-2) Schwarzer; Baird Hangeland, Hughes, Salcido: Dempsey, Murphy (Sidwell, 77) Etuhu, Duff (Davies, 81); Dembele, Zamora (Johnson, 62)

Referee: Stuart Attwell
Attendance: 25,692

Blackpool: (4-3-3) Kingson; Baptiste, Cathcart, Evatt, Crainey; Adam, Vaughan, Grandin (Puncheon, 68); Ormerod (Varney, 68), Beattie (Kornilenko, 68), Taylor-Fletcher

Miles Travelled: 0
Total Miles: 5,270

Game 34

*

Arsenal

Bloomfield Road, 10-04-11

Rather more normal preparations for this one, but again not straightforward. Craig and Rachel are heading north and a phone call around 0945 from around Warrington is a prompt to get the bacon and eggs on. Well breakfasted, Craig and I leave at 1050 on a hot, sunny morning and wisely decide the motorways may not be advisable. It proves a good call and it's busy getting into Blackpool, but we're parked up at around 1200. Craig is off to the pub whilst I set up and test the equipment before heading off round to see Matt. Just as I reach the tunnel, the Arsenal party arrives and I get the opportunity to shake hands with Arsene Wenger, a man I have revered over the years.

Matt is in top form and fills me in with all sorts of news before revealing the team. There's a major blow as David Vaughan is injured and there'll be three more changes: Keith Southern is Vaughan's replacement, Jason Puncheon for Elliot Grandin, DJ returns from suspension for James Beattie and Luke Varney starts in preference to Brett Ormerod. That

149

selection certainly looks to have more pace about it, but with Fabregas back for Arsenal, this will be one hell of a test. Summariser Paul Simpson joins me back on the other side of the ground and I pick up the programme at 1320. There's a late change to the announced Arsenal line up as keeper Manuel Almunia has hurt his knee in the warm up. 41 year old Jens Lehman will make an emotional return to the Premier League in what will be his 200th start for The Gunners and he gets a terrific reception from all sides of a packed and rocking Bloomfield Road. Blackpool start well and are definitely the better side for the first quarter of an hour ... get the feeling you've heard this one before?

1348   Abou Diaby picks up possession in his own half and strolls forward before feeding Robin Van Persie on the Arsenal left. The Dutchman cuts the ball across the box and Diaby is all alone to side-foot home ..0-1

1351   Before Pool have chance to respond, the lead is doubled. Fabregas finds Emmanuel Eboue..charging into the box and he smashes in the second 0-2

1406   Blackpool are all over the shop and Arsenal have chances aplenty to finish the job. Kingson saves well from Samir Nasri.

1406   The same Arsenal man hits the post.

1410   Diaby over elaborates and Pool scramble it away.

1415   GTF's mazy run and cross is bundled goalwards by DJ but a combination of Lehman and Laurent Koscielny scramble it away on the stroke of half-time.

1438 Charlie leads a break and finds Jason Puncheon. He slips in DJ who is flattened late by Lehman and as everybody waits for the penalty, GTF tucks home the loose ball. Blackpool are back in it ... but why was no action taken against Lehman?......................1-2

1440 The mighty Arsenal are rocking and Koscielny brings down GTF in the box for the most nailed on penalty you're ever likely to see. Referee Lee Mason is five yards away and waves play on. The uproar and pandemonium are more than justified!

1443 A rampant GTF crosses from the right, it beats Lehman but Keith Southern fails to make any contact with his head from a yard out. A massive chance slips by!

1448 Clearly worried, Arsene Wenger sends on Theo Walcott for the anonymous Andre Arshavin.

1502 Diaby frees Walcott down the right and Van Persie, from an offside position, races down the middle. Precise cross, cool finish from the Dutchman, game over...1-3

1510 The brilliant GTF isn't finished yet as he sets up DJ only for Lehman to make an excellent save – Blackpool's last chance.

1517 It's over. Pool are left to rue what might have been.

1525 In the dressing room corridor, the home door is locked and the gaffer is venting his frustrations big time.

This Is The Best Trip...

1540   Ollie emerges but immediately says to Matt that he will speak to nobody until he has been to see the referee. With the 'cooling off' period, this could be a long job!

1547   DJ Campbell gives his views on the day and says he still believes the necessary points can be gained.

1602   Eventually the officials allow the gaffer an audience.

1616   After doing TV, Matt accompanies Ollie into the office. With much shaking of the head but also an amount of calm, he gives me a six and a half minute interview to say he, like everyone else in the ground, was dumbfounded by the 'non-penalty' decision.

1645   Interviews filed, son collected, its back home – but not before crawling back along a jam packed M55. Sums up the day really!

Blackpool 1 Arsenal 3
(Taylor-Fletcher) - (Diaby, Eboue, Van Persie)

Blackpool: (4-3-3) Kingson; Baptiste, Evatt, Cathcart, Crainey; Adam, Southern (Phillips, 82), Puncheon (Kornilenko, 84); Varney (Reid, 60), Campbell, Taylor-Fletcher

Referee: Lee Mason
Attendance: 16,030

Arsenal: (4-4-2) Lehman; Eboue, Koscielny, Squillaci, Clichy; Fabregas (Ramsey, 88), Diaby, Wilshere; Arshavin (Walcott, 61); Van Persie, Nasri (Gibbs, 87)

Miles Travelled: 90
Total Miles: 5,360

Game 35

*

Wigan Athletic

Bloomfield Road, 16-04-11

Another non-straightforward morning of preparations for me ... and a painful one! During the week I've managed to tear all my abdominal muscles (I think) and moving about the house has been extremely painful. With the help of a liberal dosage of ibuprofen and generally taking it easy, I've managed to fend off numerous orders about going to the doctors. Instead my plan is to get to the ground even earlier than I usually do and see if I can grab five minutes with club physio Phil Horner.

So after driving extremely carefully, I just about manage to drag my broadcasting kit from the car to the ground and as I'm setting up, Steve Thompson is on the pitch setting out the cones for the warm up. He looks at me quizzically as I make my way down the steps and he bursts out laughing when I tell him I think I may have injured myself falling over a washing line! I make my way round to the main stand where Phil is chatting to the gaffer. I hover around until Phil is alone and ask him for some advice. Inside the treatment room he asks me when and where I get pain and instantly diagnoses 'classic hernia symptoms'. Rest is the only remedial treatment and he strongly suggests I give my workout routines a miss - perhaps a little gentle spell on my exercise bike if I have to. I thank him for his help but can't escape some stick from the home dressing room where Thommo has told the lads how I've done myself a mischief. 'Easy diagnosis Chissie - you're under the thumb. Second opinion - keep away from f...ing washing lines.' Glad I gave them a laugh - it was to prove their only one of the day! I then progressed as far as Matt's office not expecting an ounce of sympathy and I wasn't disappointed. The team shows three changes - Matt Gilks back in goal, Neal Eardley in for Bap and Elliot Grandin gets a midfield berth ahead of Jason Puncheon. Back to the broadcasting point for the start of the programme - but I have a bad feeling.

1503   Craig Cathcart makes a complete hash of a Pool free kick on half-way. Charles N'Zogbia races away and the hapless Cathcart slips on to his backside chasing Hugo Rodellega. Clean in, the striker nutmegs Gillo and rolls it into the corner 0-1

1543   It has taken a very poor Blackpool until two minutes from half time to muster a shot at goal. Even then Keith Southern fails to trouble Ali Al-Habsi.

1545   Elliot Grandin's long range header is an easy first save of the game for the Wigan keeper.

1546   Pool take a sloppy throw in and N'Zobgia drifts away from Charlie, rounds two defenders and passes the ball beyond Matt Gilks. That just about summed up a dreadful first half.............................0-2

1614   The gaffer's frustration is summed up by a triple change…Phillips, Puncheon and Beattie enter the fray for Grandin, Varney and Fletch.

1617   No change in the course of the game as Gillo saves well from man of the match, N'Zogbia.

1622   It's all over now. Mohammed Diame isn't closed down and his low drive hits Neal Eardley on the backside and flies in past a helpless Gilks..............0-3

1640   Eards blasts a free kick into the Wigan wall. The ball breaks to Matt Phillips whose low cross is turned in by DJ. It's nothing to affect the result and, in truth, not much consolation 1-3

1649   Peter Walton ends the torture in front of a half empty Bloomfield. What a tortuous afternoon!

1720   Matt brings Ollie in for the interviews. He's not a happy camper and blasts whoever was responsible for showing Pool's goals at Wigan on the big screen before the game. 'That showed a lack of respect. I can remember us scoring four, but I also remember that Wigan had chances as well and that we had more than our fair share of luck on the day'. He rues horrible defensive errors and also has a pop at the fans telling them to criticise him not the players. Defiantly, the gaffer retains a belief that they can still stay up and heaps praise on his mate Roberto Martinez. 'Good luck to him, he plays the game the right way'.

1735   A bitterly disappointed DJ admits the lads let

themselves down badly and blames his lack of sharpness for not converting some half chances. 'We've got to be better than that and we will be.'

1750 I trudge back to the car having just witnessed the worst performance - and result - of the season. This is not the time to be below the dreaded line for the first time in the campaign. It's not been a good day

---

Blackpool 1 Wigan 3
(Campbell) - (Rodellega, N'Zogbia, Eardley o.g.)

Blackpool: (4-3-3) Gilks; Eardley, Evatt, Cathcart, Crainey; Southern, Adam, Grandin (Phillips, 57); Taylor-Fletcher (Beattie, 57), Campbell, Varney (Puncheon, 57)

Referee: Peter Walton
Attendance: 16,030

Wigan: (4-4-2) Al-Habsi; Boyce, Caldwell, Alcaraz, Gohouri; McCarthy, Diame (Gomez, 80), Watson, N'Zogbia; Cleverley, Rodellega

Miles Travelled: 90
Total Miles: 5,450

Game 36

*

Newcastle United

Bloomfield Road, 23-04-11

A home game on Easter Saturday always brings major traffic problems but given the recent hot spell, today bears all the hallmarks of being a nightmare. The only solution is an extra early start to ensure the coast bound traffic is negated. No chance of me using the motorways either so I'm already on my way via Preston and Riversway by 1015. Exactly an hour later I'm parked up and being of a superstitious nature and knowing that Blackpool desperately need a result, I head down to the world famous promenade for a stroll.

As previously mentioned, Pool generally do well when I go for a nerve settling walk and as anticipated, the bars are full of Geordies in good voice and well lubricated even at that hour. Back to the car park to collect the kit and I'm at the point setting up at around noon. Mick Lowes and John Anderson from BBC Newcastle are already installed as I try - and fail - to connect to the studio. After several changes of leads and re-booting the equipment, the magic red and green lights appear to end an extremely stressful half hour. I eventually get round to the other side of the ground to seek out physio Phil Horner. I give him a bottle of wine for his time and diagnosis last week and he checks on my recovery process. He gives me a cautious green light to resume my exercise programme but a 'take it easy' warning is also issued. Phil also reveals today's team and after 35 games, I've finally second-guessed the gaffer by picking the exact eleven. Vaughny is back from injury to replace Elliot Grandin, Bap is recalled at the expense of young Craig Cathcart and there's a rare start for Matt Phillips with 'Reg' Varney dropping to the bench. I like the look of that ! Next off to the media room where the testosterone levels are sky high – if the lads reach a similar level on the pitch we'll be fine. Back at the press box, Andy Bayes opens the show at 1400 and the banter is good right up to kick off time.

1507   Newcastle keeper Tim Krul rolls the ball out on the left and Jose Enrique pokes it further forward to Joey Barton on the touch line, right in front of the commentary point. Gateshead born Keith Southern sees Barton attempting to turn and thunders in with a bone jarring - but entirely fair - challenge. You could hear the wind disappearing from Barton's lungs as he bounced once on the pitch side before ending in a crumpled heap on the advertising boards. It's the clearest of statements from Southern and was to prove a total reflection of Blackpool's approach on the day.

1509   Fletch is close to an opener but his shot goes wide.

1515   The same man is inches away from converting a wonderful cross from Stephen Crainey as Blackpool start with real purpose.

1516   A loose pass from Charlie is picked up by Joey
       Barton who instantly releases Peter Lovenkrands to
       hammer a shot past Matt Gilks. Here we go again!
      0-1

1530   DJ goes down under a challenge from keeper Tim
       Krul but Martin Atkinson waves away Pool's second
       penalty shout. Replays show he was correct to do so.

1531   Charlie whips in a corner to the near post and it flies
       goalbound off DJ's thigh. Jose Enrique leaves his
       post to head away but the linesman flags
       immediately that it had crossed the line.................1-1

1531   It's all Blackpool and Ian Evatt dribbles into the box.
       Danny Simpson slips and handles the ball on the
       deck TWICE. A stone-wall penalty - waved away.

1547   As Blackpool leave the pitch at half-time the whole
       crowd are on their feet applauding.

1639   A Charlie Adam daisy-cutter smashes back off Krul's
       left hand post.

1626   Newcastle substitute Stephen Ireland flashes a shot
       wide in a rare break by the Geordies.

1643   Substitute Luke Varney is just wide with what
       proves to be Blackpool's last of many fine chances.

1730   Everybody wants a piece of Keith Southern it seems.
       TV, national press and last of all today, ourselves.
       The born and bred Geordie gives his usual honest
       and unassuming assessment and generates a real

belief that Pool can survive. He plays down his early clash with Barton who, in fairness, simply shrugged it off and got on with it. 'The lads wanted to dig in today and that's the way I've always played.' I didn't need the confirmation...Keith Southern would be in my team week in, week out.

1755   Walking back to the car is a totally different experience than a week ago. The lads were brilliant today and other results have gone Blackpool's way. But having totally outplayed the Geordies, a return of one point leaves me feeling short changed. By one goal, Pool have hauled themselves above the line and as I begin the drive to home town Barrow, the various permutations begin swimming round my head. My word, it's going to be some month ahead!

Blackpool 1 Newcastle 1
(Campbell) - (Lovenkrands)

Blackpool: 4-3-3) Gilks; Eardley, Evatt, Baptiste, Crainey; Southern, Vaughan, Adam; Phillips (Varney, 83), Campbell, Taylor-Fletcher (Puncheon, 88)

Newcastle: (4-4-2) Krul; Simpson, Coloccini, Williamson, Jose Enrique; Barton, Tiote, Nolan (Perch, 86), Guttierrez; Ameobi (Kuqi, 90), Lovenkrands (Ireland, 62)

Referee: Martin Atkinson
Attendance: 16,006

Miles Travelled: 90
Total Miles: 5,540

Game 37

*

Stoke City

Bloomfield Road, 30-04-11

Another Bank Holiday weekend means the potential of traffic problems especially as this unseasonably hot and sunny spell continues. But first, the hernia is healing and I'm back on the exercise bike first thing, catching up on last night's TV Super League.

I'm breakfasted and ready to go by 1100 with the local traffic news encouraging for my route across Preston. Apart from a short delay at the level crossing in Rufford, the journey is trouble free and I pull into the car park at exactly the same time as former BBC Five Live commentator Ron Jones. He's driven up from his Cardiff home to do the game for Irish station Today FM and also reported his delight that his drive was painless. He's glad I arrived when I did - he hasn't been to Bloomfield Road for 20 years and he welcomes some local knowledge and advice as we walk to the ground together. Ron gets the usual Keith Graham welcome and as we set up the equipment, Five Live's John Murray is already recording some pieces - this game is the main commentary game nationally as well. BBC TV's *Match of the Day* main man, Jonathon Pearce is here as well and as we both walk round to the dressing room area, Jonathon bombards me with Pool related questions. I'm confident the gaffer will stick with the side who played so well last week and Jonathon's next line of questioning concerns positional details, shape etc. Blackpool's club photographer Baz spots us together in the tunnel and takes a couple of shots of us sharing notes before I venture into the media room. Team confirmed, I'm off to see Matt who is sorting tickets out for Phil and Thommo. All three are chipper and upbeat and speaking to one or two of the lads as they arrive, it's clear that last week's performance has done them a power of good.

Our sports programme has started early today with Burnley kicking off at Leeds at 1245, so I'm needed at the point at around 1330, half time in that game. Preview done, I'm then free to go back over to the other side so I take my camera with me. I'm aware that it's Charlie's penultimate game at Bloomfield and I want a photo taken with him. Good enough, Charlie obliges and I thank him for all he's done for the club. I'm in the tunnel area when Stoke emerge for their warm up. As they file past, I knew that they were big, but in the flesh they are HUGE. This is going to be a real physical examination against the FA Cup finalists. By the time I'm back to the press box, summariser Paul Simpson is already in place and the 20 minutes or so between the end of the Burnley game and kick off flies by.

1508   After a bright start when GTF, DJ and Vaughny have - and reject - chances to shoot, Matt Phillips does fire goalwards, but mis-hits and the ball dribbles wide.

1520   As we go round the grounds, Simmo gently points out to me that for some inexplicable reason, I've spent the first 20 minutes referring to the Stoke skipper as David Shawcross instead of Ryan! I correct my mistake and offer apoligies…is senility finally setting in?

1537　Stephen Crainey's excellent cross is brilliantly headed up and over his own bar by Robert Huth.

1545　The defining moment of the afternoon. David Vaughan takes a sloppy throw in between Eards and Bap. Glen Whelan nips in to free Kenwyne Jones who rounds the advancing Matt Gilks and as Ian Evatt slips in trying to recover, Jones controls the ball and steadies himself. As I scream 'goal, it's 1-0 to Stoke', the big man slices five yards wide of the gaping goal. What an astonishing howler and Mark Clattenberg blows for half-time shaking his head in disbelief.

1613　Glen Whelan's goal bound 20 yarder is pushed away by Matt Gilks for his only save of the match.

1629　The gaffer pushes for a winner by sending on Reg and Sergei Kornilenko for Matty Phillips and a very tired Fletch.

1637　Sergei gets on the end of a Charlie Adam cross but Asimir Begovic saves his header easily. In a game of very few chances, this proves to be the last one.

1705　The gaffer is out and about quickly and there's laughter in the corridor as he and Matt approach the office. There's plenty of banter - some of it very risqué surrounding the Royal Wedding - before we switch on the machine. Ollie is delighted that his side stood up to the anticipated physical challenge and describes Evo and Bap as outstanding. His only regret is that 'one or two of his more creative players weren't quite at their best' and so the team were unable to break Stoke down. It's pretty clear he meant Charlie, Vaughny and DJ who, despite not being at the top of their game, still tried their socks off. The gaffer jokes that he's paid Kenwyne Jones to miss that chance and finishes by re-stating his belief that his team can pick up points 'where nobody expects them to'.

1720 Ian Evatt comes into the interview room in bullish mood. 'Before we start let me tell you…that was a big point gained. If we beat Bolton, we'll stay up. 38 points will do'. He repeats all of that on microphone and says that's the genuine belief of all the lads in the dressing room. He's delighted to have been praised by his gaffer and says the game was exactly what he'd expected.

1740 All duties completed, it's time for that reflective walk back to the car. Another home game without a win and those key four consecutive April home games produced just two points. But still Pool are above that dreaded line by virtue of a one goal better goal difference than Wigan. Rivals Wolves and West Ham play on the Sunday and a win for either will see Blackpool in the bottom three. It'll be another Sunday glued to a radio with everything completely crossed but tonight, I think I can manage a beer.

Blackpool 0 Stoke 0

-

Blackpool: (4-3-3) Gilks; Eardley, Evatt, Baptiste, Crainey; Southern, Vaughan, Adam; Phillips (Varney, 72), Campbell, Taylor-Fletcher (Kornilenko, 72)

Stoke City: (4-4-2) Begovic; Wilkinson (Shotton, 56), Huth, Shawcross, Wilson; Pennant (Diao, 90) Whelan, Whitehead, Delap (Carew, 81); Jones, Walters

Miles Travelled: 90
Total Miles: 5,630

Referee: Mark Clattenberg
Attendance: 16,003

Game 38

*

Tottenham Hotspur

White Hart Lane, 07-05-11

B y now you'll have gathered that I like to be early and prepared in plenty of time but, even by my own standards, this should top the lot. This game is the late TV game on Saturday at 1730 ... my preparations start at 1315 on Thursday afternoon! Jan and I are off to London for a long weekend to take in much more than the match. The drive down to Craig and Rachel's is painless and Thursday evening sees us share an excellent meal. I spend Friday sightseeing in the capital before meeting up with Jan and second son Dean outside The Theatre Royal in Drury Lane.

It's the first preview night of *Shrek: The Musical* and Dean is slightly nervous. I'm not exactly over excited about his latest show but, in the end, thoroughly enjoy the evening. We stay at girlfriend Jenna's flat and drive back round to Craig's on the Saturday morning. I manage to watch him playing cricket for an hour or so before setting sail - by train - for White Hart Lane. Thankfully it's fine for the 15 minute walk down Park Lane and I cast an anxious eye at the TV for the scorelines on arrival at about 1520. West Ham are losing at home to Blackburn and Ashley Young has just equalized for Villa at home to Wigan. I get to the radio point which is just ten yards behind the dug outs and way surpasses Goodison Park as easily the most cramped in the Premier League. The media conditions are totally out of context with the rest of the fantastic stadium. Just as I complete the usual checks the team arrive and Ian Evatt tells me that there will be one change - big Sergei Kornilenko replaces Matt Phillips. Back in the press room, sweet and sour chicken is more than pleasant as the results come in. West Ham get a late equalizer and both games with impact for Blackpool end in 1-1 draws. Wigan's point sends Pool back below the relegation line so everybody knows something is required from the game. It's a huge ask.

1743   Gareth Bale's low shot is turned away for a corner.

1747   Master blocker Ian Evatt comes up with a huge effort to deny Jermaine Defoe from 12 yards.

1753   Blackpool had been lively and Heurelho Gomes brilliantly saves a close range volley from Charlie, not that the listeners to BBC Radio Lancashire knew anything about it. I was blissfully unaware that we had been knocked off air by a late arrival in the afore-mentioned cramped press box. Both Steve Canavan and I have obeyed the radio station's rules and switched off our mobile phones (they interfere with the output) and with the late afternoon sun shining on our equipment, we failed to spot that the red and green lights had gone out on the ISDN. Frantic notes came to us from Matt and Mek from the media team, but it was a full ten minutes before contact was restored and with it, profuse apologies.

This Is The Best Trip...

1754　Blackpool force a corner and from Charlie's delivery Sergei Kornilenko puts a free header over the bar when he should have at least hit the target.

1755　Back to the other end and Gillo denies Rafael van der Vaart an opener.

1803　Bale rips in a daisy cutter which screams just wide.

1816　Half-time arrives with the scoreline blank - quite how is difficult to fathom.

1832　Jason Puncheon replaces an off the pace Kornilenko as the second half begins. Spurs replace Roman Pavlyuchenko with Aaron Lennon.

1834　Spurs are fired up now and van der Vaart blazes a great chance over the bar.

1834　Bale follows suite when well placed.

1843　The Welsh winger ruins a great run with a wild high finish as Pool are really under the cosh.

1845　In a rare Blackpool raid David Vaughan shaves the post from 20 yards.

1853　A key moment as Bale and Keith Southern tussle for possession on the touchline. Charlie comes in and catches Bale's ankle. It looks innocuous to the naked eye but replays show it to be a real bad tackle, more out of timing that malice. The Players' Player of the Year is stretchered off to be replaced by Peter Crouch.

1904   Cue three minutes of mayhem. DJ should open the
        scoring, but from ten yards he allows Gomes to push
        it away for a corner.

1905   Charlie swings it in and, inexplicably, Michael
        Dawson handles to give away a penalty. Charlie
        drives it low to the left of Gomes who saves
        brilliantly. Refusing to let disappointment get the
        better of him, Charlie charges after the ball as
        Gomes celebrates with star jumps.

1906   In comes the corner, Gomes flaps at it and in chasing
        his effort, bundles over Fletch. Lee Probert points to
        the spot again as Charlie runs 70 yards up the pitch
        to grab the ball. He's on the edge of his own box
        when he tucks it firmly under his arm. DJ has run
        back as far as half way and from the body language,
        it's obvious he wants to take the second penalty.
        After words between skipper and striker bring no
        change to the possession of the ball, DJ begins to try
        and physically wrestle the ball away from Charlie.
        Equally, the Scot is having none of it in a scene
        rapidly resembling a primary school playground as
        he marches towards the spot pointing to his chest.
        Ian Evatt drags a distraught DJ out of the way as
        Charlie eventually spots the ball up. There'll be no
        placement this time as the left foot hammer smashes
        it past the Brazilian keeper in a blur of sheer power.
        Charlie is submerged by his team mates with the
        exception of one. A still tormented DJ has to be
        soothed as he makes his way back to the re-start.
        What an astonishing display from the little man in
        what was an incredible passage of play, but
        Blackpool have a precious lead 0-1

This Is The Best Trip...

1911   Tottenham are piling it on but a be-calmed DJ leads
       a Pool break. He cleverly gets Punch in but his short
       is dragged wide.

1912   That big chance to seal a vital win is punished in
       cruel fashion when Defoe thumps in the equaliser1-1

1915   Six minutes of stoppage time see Blackpool gold
       medalists in time wasting, but a point is enough to
       lift them above Wigan again. In every sense this has
       been an amazing game of football.

1935   Matt brings the gaffer pitch side and once again he
       is bursting with pride as he commends the way his
       team handled themselves on the night. He jokes that
       he'll have a fued to sort out on the coach home
       regarding the Charlie-DJ spat. He says he thought
       DJ should have had the second penalty but praises
       the bottle and confidence of his skipper. 'Those two
       had an agreement from the training ground that
       should Charlie miss one then DJ would have the
       next.' Ollie then blasted Alan Shearer for last week's
       TV comments about Charlie. *Match of the Day* had
       highlighted a series of recent mistakes made by
       Charlie and Shearer had suggested that he hoped
       Adam's time hadn't passed him by. It was a clear
       inference that having been denied his big move in
       the transfer window, the opportunity might not
       come round again. 'Al won't be getting a Christmas
       card from me after that. Come on...the lad is only at
       the beginning of his career, he'll go on to be a super
       star. Your time's passed you by Al, that's why you
       sit in that studio. Don't upset my skipper like that!'

1945   Charlie appears from the tunnel and admits he changed his mind for the first penalty and explains why he charged off in search of the ball for the second. 'I knew DJ wanted it but there was no way I wasn't going to have it. These things happen and it just shows how much DJ cares. He's a man and he'll accept it. It's gone now, we'll get ready for a huge game with Bolton.' I ask if he will be buying DJ a drink tonight but the skipper swerves it, replying that although both he and DJ were staying down in London they would be going their separate ways. Interestingly enough more than one or two of the Monday tabloids were to carry a story of the gaffer having to intervene between the two on the coach home. Is that what they call journalistic licence? Neither Charlie or DJ were anywhere near the coach!

Spurs 1 Blackpool 1
(Defoe) - (Adam, pen)

Tottenham H: (4-4-2) Gomes; Kaboul, Dawson, Gallas, Rose (Kranjcar, 90), van der Vaart, Modric, Sandro, Bale (Crouch, 64); Defoe, Pavlyuchenko (Lennon, 46)

Blackpool: (4-3-3) Gilks; Eardley (Beattie, 90), Baptiste, Evatt, Crainey; Southern, Adam, Vaughan; Taylor-Fletcher (Cathcart, 77), Kornilenko (Puncheon, 46), Campbell

Referee:Lee Probert
Attendance: 35,585

Miles Travelled: 460
Total Miles: 6,090

Game 39

Bolton Wanderers
Bloomfield Road, 14-05-11

F A Cup Final day in England and for the first time in living memory there are other football fixtures. Yes I know it's ludicrous but this must win game for Blackpool is one of four Premier League games scheduled to kick off at 1245. I'm awake bright and early and I can't escape the thought that Blackpool could be relegated by mid afternoon. A loss at Bloomfield coupled with a Wolves victory at Sunderland and that would be that, ending many weeks of what if's, and numerous permutations and calculations.

I'm not much company over breakfast and I decide to leave for the seaside just before 1000. The journey across Preston is without problem and I'm at a very blustery Blackpool in just under an hour. BBC Radio Five Live reporter Peter Slater and Steve Roberts from Today FM are there already and I get some gentle stick about the state of my nerves. Sports boss Gary Hickson is presenting from the ground and as I do a line check Jon Lowe tells me that my summariser will be former Pool striker Andy Preece ...

excellent! All checks done, I'm off to the main stand to dig out the team news. If everyone's fit and healthy, for me it will be a matter of who starts instead of Sergei Kornilenko. I suspect it might be Matt Phillips but it's Jason Puncheon who did well from the bench at Spurs, who gets the nod. The lads are bombarding Matt and the media team for tickets – Charlie, Bap and big Evo are desperate, but Evo sticks around long enough to confirm what he said after the last home game. 'We'll beat these today and that will be enough.' I love his confidence and faith in the opponents of the other relegation strugglers! Out in the corridor, Bolton are arriving and I bump into one of my former summarisers, coach Steve Davis. He asks how I've enjoyed the season and heaps praise on the way Pool have gone about it. I can't help asking him not to end it here and now before going across to meet Gary. There's real anxiety as big Preecy hasn't shown yet – but he is an ex-footballer so we should expect him to be late! Sure enough, wearing a big smile he takes his place between us and we're good to go.

1251   Blackpool's excellent start is blown as Kevin Davies volleys Bolton's first chance past Gillo...................0-1

1254   Charlie gets DJ in behind Gretaar Steinson and the little man lifts an excellent equaliser over Jussi Jaaskelainen 1-1

1303   Wanderers defender Paul Robinson heads a Pool corner against his own bar.

1304   Pool's incessant pressure pays as Jason Puncheon fires home from 18 yards 2-1

1309   Bolton level it up on a rare raid. Ricardo Gardner

feeds Matthew Taylor and his left footer is across the face of Matt Gilks and goes in off the inside of the post...2-2

1315 The melting pot boils over. Zat Knight has a grounded Fletch by the throat and suddenly all the players except Gillo are involved in the ensuing melee. Yellow cards are issued to the initial combatants.

1325 Kevin Davies rattles Blackpool's crossbar as chances continue at both ends.

1331 The Adam-Campbell partnership comes up trumps again. Charlie's sumptuous left wing cross is touched in at the back stick and Bloomfield Road erupts to celebrate a half-time lead.........................3-2

1355 Speculation that Blackpool might hold on lasts just seven second half minutes. Winger Chung Yong Lee skips past Matt Gilks on the bye-line and stands up a cross for Daniel Sturridge to nudge over the line 3-3...

1406 In typical Blackpool fashion, Bolton are caught over committed up field. Charlie leads a four against three break and slips a pass to Fletch on the left. He returns the compliment just inside the box and the Blackpool skipper curls in an absolute picture book goal...4-3

1424 Brett and James Beattie replace Punch and GTF as Pool look relatively comfortable in charge of their lead.

1430 A very tired Charlie is replaced by Craig Cathcart and the skipper, probably bidding the club farewell on his home ground, receives a rapturous standing ovation.

1437 Andre Marriner brings Blackpool's Premier League season at Bloomfield Road to an end and Pool will take their survival campaign to the last day at Old Trafford against the Champions, Manchester United.

1457 The players, staff and their families come out to do a season ending lap of honour. As they receive a fantastic reception, it dawns that other results today will probably mean that Blackpool will have to win at the Theatre of Dreams to stay up. No problem then!

1505 Amidst the din, I grab a few words with Ian Evatt who jokes that Sir Alex might select himself next week to make the task easier.

1510 The gaffer is ready and waiting and begins the interview with a laugh and a 'dear, oh dear, oh dear … would you believe it?' He's realistic and hugely proud whatever the eventual outcome will be. 'We want a party too next week.'

1520 DJ comes in and emphasizes the togetherness in the camp rather than bigging up his goals.

1545 My interviews are filed and also one with Karl Oyston done by Gary. The chairman admits to have felt physically sick for most of the afternoon.

1600   I begin the drive home listening to the second half of
        a less than inspiring FA Cup Final. I can't help
        feeling robbed by that Wolves victory at Sunderland.
        Ah, well, miracles do happen don't they?

Blackpool 4 Bolton 3
(Campbell 2, Puncheon, Adam) - (Davies, Taylor, Sturridge)

Blackpool: (4-3-3) Gilks; Eardley, Evatt, Baptiste, Crainey; Adam (Cathcart, 87), Vaughan, Southern; Taylor-Fletcher (Beattie, 81), Campbell, Puncheon (Ormerod, 81)	Bolton: (4-4-2) Jaaskelainen; Steinson, Cahill, Knight, Robinson: Lee, Muamba (Cohen, 50), Gardner (Klasnic, 78) Taylor; Sturridge, Davies (Moreno, 83)
Referee: Andre Marriner Attendance: 15,979	Miles travelled: 90 Total Miles: 6,180

Sunday May 15th
No this isn't a double-header weekend for Blackpool, but it
is a matchday for me. I'm on rugby league duties for BBC
Radio Merseyside and have a trip to Dewsbury v Widnes ...
I get all the good gigs! But the day does merit some column
inches in that it's the day when the other clubs in the
relegation mix complete their penultimate fixtures and, in so
doing, they'll frame the equations for the season's final
fixtures next Sunday. The game in Yorkshire is a really
entertaining affair but I can't wait to get into the car for the
scores that really matter. Fulham are ahead at Birmingham
... could this season's Carling Cup winners be dragged right
into the relegation mix? I also applaud the score from the
DW Stadium ... West Ham are two up at Wigan in a game
where a draw would probably be the best result for Pool.

176

So I'm in the car just after half-time in the Five Live commentary game which kicked off at 1600 and the news is still good. Fulham are two up at Birmingham and my in-grained mental goal difference calculator tells me that one more goal for The Cottagers will lift Blackpool out of the bottom three on goals scored ... come on you whites! Then Wigan score and that draw I've been hunting looks on. One becomes two at the DW and the 2 – 2 scoreline will be enough to send the Hammers down. Finished at St Andrews at 2 – 0 and that same mental calculator of mine tells me that Blackpool will begin the final game below the line – but Birmingham have to go to Spurs, themselves pushing for fifth place in the division which brings qualification for the Europa League. If they lose by more than Pool do at the Theatre of Dreams, the Seasiders can afford to be beaten and still stay up.

How the hell I'm concentrating on my driving I do not know. I'm just crossing Saddleworth Moor back into God's Own Country when commentator Darren Fletcher announces there'll be four minutes of stoppages at Wigan. Both teams have been throwing caution to the wind seeking a winner which I definitely don't want, particularly a Wigan one. I check on the car clock and look again four minutes later – come on ref ... blow it, blow it! Then, well beyond time a defining moment – not for West Ham for whom a draw is not enough to prevent relegation – but for Roberto Martinez and his men. Their best player by a long way, Charles N'Zogbia, fires a winner for The Latics to send the fans into delirium.

The final whistle follows immediately and West Ham are the first club to be relegated. Wigan's win finalises the equation facing Blackpool on the last day. Ollie's side must match or better Wigan's result at Stoke and hope that Spurs beat Birmingham by more than United beat Blackpool by.

This Is The Best Trip...

Lancashire neighbours Blackburn Rovers, themselves not out of danger, could also help if they can beat Wolves by three or more at Molineux. Simple then ... Pool could lose and stay up, or win and go down. Absolutely crazy!

Friday May 20th

Again, it's no match day but it is the start of the most vital weekend of the season and who should I be out in the company of this evening ... none other than the gaffer himself. It's club secretary Matt's annual cricket club sportsman's dinner, and Ollie is honouring a promise to his mate by agreeing to be the principal speaker. Given the circumstances, I'm certain that Mr Holloway would have preferred a slightly lower profile beginning to the big weekend, but this deal was struck a long time ago and it's clear that Ollie is a man of his word.

Matt has invited Jan and me to this event for the past four years and a spartan text informs us to be at the very up-market Norton Grange Hotel in Castleton for a 1900 champagne reception. Ollie and Kim are already in the VIP zone, and charged with glasses of bubbles, we go over for a chat. I've taken a calculated gamble by wearing the wonderfully outrageous striped shirt that Dean and Jenna bought me for Christmas and, sure enough, the gaffer doesn't disappoint. 'My God Chizzers, that's a wicked old shirt son' and he proceeds to do a full 360 degree inspection.

'You look great in that pal, scrubs up well doesn't he love?' As the compliments continue, I know I'll be in for some grief when he has a microphone in hand. I then upset him big time by reminding him Mike Dean is to referee the United game as the two have 'previous' from earlier on in the season but he's soon back on form as the evening's events begin.

As ever at the Shaw Dinner ... or generally anywhere

in life really ... Matt, armed with microphone, takes the piss out of all and sundry and with a profusion of alcohol, the night flies by until it's time for the top of the bill. Ollie gets up to a tremendous reception and it's not long before my shirt gets the inevitable mention. 'Old Chizzers has come as Josesph look' ... and he then proceeds to launch into a rendition of 'Any Dream Will Do' which brings the house down. It's nearer 0100 in the morning than midnight when someone finally prises the microphone out of his hands to tumultuous applause. I manage to catch him as he leaves to wish him well for the final time before Sunday. He genuinely believes Pool will stay up – what a top man!

Game 40

*

Manchester United

Old Trafford, 22-05-11

They've been calling it 'Survival Sunday' for months and wasn't it always going to come down to this? A visit to one of the giants of world football on a day when they are to be crowned Champions...what a way to finish a season! United's point at Blackburn last week clinched the title whilst Blackpool ended last Saturday below the line and knowing that they would probably need to do what nobody else had managed this season, win at Old Trafford. Even then, that might not be enough to see them survive.

Matchday preparations for me begin with an alarm call at 0610 ... yes, ten past six in the morning! BBC Radio Five Live had contacted me on Friday to ask if I would go live on air into their Sunday morning breakfast show along with Mark Regan from BBC West Midlands. The angle was a geographical one - three of the five clubs fighting for survival are from the North West and the other two from the West Midlands listening area. Villa fan Phil Williams asks the questions and Mark and I are both careful with our responses, predicting nothing which could upset anybody! We wish each other well and I'm back in bed by half past six … not much chance of any more sleep though. The world of 'what if's' is spinning round my well active brain and I have to be strong not to start looking back at what might have been over the course of the season. I'm up and about by 0900 and I give the broadcasting equipment a final check over … that must be twenty checks since last weekend. Conversation is sparse and after a light breakfast I'm off to Trafford Park around 1130.

The traffic is as busy as anticipated over the Barton Bridge, but eases once the punters have poured into The Trafford Centre …is there a counter attraction on somewhere? It's testimony to my state of mind that I contrive to take a wrong turning on a route which I should be able to manage in my sleep, but soon the magnificence of the stadium looms on the horizon and the mere sight of it suddenly brings a chilling reality to the situation. Fancy having to come here needing something to survive, and as I am running these thoughts through my mind, I wonder how my emotions will be on the return journey in seven hours or so. As ever, the car park stewards at Old Trafford are excellent, and a brief flash of my Premier League pass sees me waved straight in to park up behind The Stretford End.

The weather men had predicted heavy showers and they weren't wrong so I wait until one particularly heavy bout of precipitation passes by. Five Live's build up has been on for half an hour or so and seemingly every caller, on whatever subject, has a good luck message for Blackpool. There are even Preston fans … and Manchester United for that matter … wanting Blackpool to win. Once the shower has passed, I unload the kit and head for the Munich Tunnel and media entrance. The Blackpool coach has arrived and I greet kit man Walesy and video analyst Liam unloading the team paraphernalia. Both shout a response which is lost in the throng of fans who queue outside the players entrance for hours on end. By 1245 I'm outside the media entrance which is firmly locked until 1300. Former Blackpool player Tony Rodwell arrives to carry out his Press Association duties for the world's press and at one o'clock on the dot, the doors open and we enter the portals of The Theatre of Dreams. I head straight for the press box itself and set up and test the ISDN. All fine and dandy and as I head back to the media suite, I take a call from Gary Hickson to say he'll be there in ten minutes or so.

Little to be done as the good and great of the football media arrive then but to try and digest a nervous lunch and watch the clock tick by ... slowly, slowly, slowly until kick off time approaches. Matt arrives with news that Pool will be the same again with a bench packed with strikers. The talk all week has been that Sir Alex will rest some of his stars ahead of the Champions League Final ... none of it. The team sheets arrive and the likes of Van der Sar, Vidic, Scholes and Berbatov will all start. The bench isn't shabby either – Rooney, Ferdinand, Owen et al. – what a task ahead as the biggest afternoon of the season gets underway in bright sunshine.

1600 ...and 22 secs. Charlie raids down the left and cuts it back for Keith Southern 12 yards out. Gnashers only needs to put his laces through it and Blackpool will have a first-minute lead. Inexplicably, Southern goes for a placed finish and skews it horribly wide.

1604 Matt Gilks beats away a sweet volley from Rafael.

1606 Blackpool are full of enterprise and Fletch could have done better than shoot wide.

1606   End to end stuff as Gillo denies Dimitar Berbatov.

1621   United break the deadlock after a mix-up between
        big Evo and keeper Gilks. Ji Sung Park pokes home
        the opener 1- 0

1629   Berbatov misses a great chance to double the lead.

1640   Pool earn a free kick close to the edge of the box. It's
        very central and Charlie curls it in away to Van der
        Sar's left for a spectacular equaliser. As scores stand,
        Blackpool are above the line 1-1

1644   Half-time arrives and everybody in this cauldron
        wants the game to end here and now. United will
        still maintain their unbeaten home record and
        Blackpool will survive. If only!

1713   Jason Puncheon and David Vaughan combine on the
        right and GTF clips Vaughny's ball past Van der Sar.
        Blackpool CAN'T be ahead, can they? Wigan are still
        goalless at Stoke, Wolves are losing at home to
        Blackburn and Birmingham are behind at Spurs.
        Let's go home ... NOW!..1-2

1719   Anderson equalizes with an unstoppable effort...
        but it's as you were elsewhere and a point would
        keep Blackpool up 2-2

1720   Michael Owen replaces Park in what could be his
        final appearance for United. How he would mark it.

1731   Disaster! Ian Evatt diverts a right wing cross past
        Gilks for an own goal of massive proportions. Before

Pool can digest the implications, a double blow from The Potteries and London. Hugo Rodellega has headed Wigan into the lead and Birmingham have equalized at Tottenham. Blackpool now have to not only equalize, but push for an unlikely victory.....3-2

1732   Down on the touch line, the gaffer knows the story of an incredible afternoon and Matt Phillips and Reg Varney replace a shot GTF and Jason Puncheon.

1734   Only a world class block from Van der Sar denies a distraught Ian Evatt an equaliser.

1737   The dream is finally shattered as Michael Owen goes clear of a bedraggled defence to hammer home the fourth 4-2

1747   Varney's header thumps back off the bar but the players, staff and over 3,000 fans know that these moments are the last rites in the Premier League.

1749   Mike Dean's whistle to end it all leads to a huge out-pouring of emotions. 'We are the Champions'rings out but quickly subsides as the heartbroken players and staff move to their fans away to my right. 75,000 people chant 'Blackpool, Blackpool.' Ian Evatt is in tears and is barely consolable by the Pool supporters belting out 'There's only one Ian Evatt!'

1755   As the preparations to present the Premier League trophy begin, I'm in a group of press people being ushered down to the tunnel entrance. The din is incredible and is maintained throughout the presentation and subsequent lap of honour.

1825   Matt brings Ian Holloway down the tunnel but any chance of an interview is drowned out by the hullabaloo. Matt and the gaffer disappear behind the scenes to find the interview theatre leaving Steve Canavan and myself to fight the crowds to get back upstairs - no easy task I can tell you.

1830   A tad breathless, but I'm there to meet the gaffer who is clearly devastated. But, as ever, he gives a frank and candid eight minute interview finishing with a magnificent touch. Typically, he doesn't duck the big question. He's already said that this group will now break up as his big hitters will be snapped up. So I take my life in my hands and ask him if he'll still be around to start the re-building work. The reply is typically Ollie - 'I'll have to sit down with my chairman and discuss where we both want to take this football club' and, almost in the same breath, quips that he'll need to get down to B&Q and start buying cement for the re-building. I've concluded the interview when Ollie asks to say one final thing ... 'I'd like to congratulate the managers of the three clubs to survive the day'. Now that takes a real man to do that in such circumstances.

1845   Interviews filed and all is just about done. Incredibly, United's players are still out on the Old Trafford pitch. Gazza thanks me for my efforts this season and I thank him for being more than fair in giving me as much of Blackpool as he could, despite his deal with Blackburn falling through. As I leave the stadium and head for the car, somehow I can't bring myself to be feeling anything like sad. The season has been every inch the fairytale that I thought it would be - a calender year straight out of Fantasy Island. The mobile phone is rammed with messages of sympathy and pride. My club may have gone down but they have won the hearts of the nation. Stick that chest out Chisnall, it's been a privilege to be a part of it.

Manchester Utd 4 Blackpool 2
(Park, Anderson, Evatt o.g. Owen) - (Adam, Taylor-Fletcher)

Man Utd: (4-4-2) Van der Sar; Rafael (Smalling, 46) Vidic (Rooney, 84), Evans, Evra; Fletcher, Scholes, Anderson; Nani, Berbatov, Park (Owen, 63)

Blackpool (4-3-3) Gilks; Eardley, Evatt, Baptiste, Crainey; Southern, Vaughan, Adam; Puncheon (Phillips, 76) Campbell, Taylor-Fletcher (Varney, 76)

Referee: Mike Dean
Attendance: 75,400

Miles Travelled: 90
Total Miles: 6,270

Monday May 23rd

Just what you want the day after you've suffered the most cruel relegation in living memory ... the club's end of season awards night dinner. In best bib and tucker, I'm at Bloomfield for the champagne reception in the board room at 1900 and I arrive in the dressing room corridor just as the lads are all assembling. I make a bee-line for Ian Evatt to commiserate with him and the big man is still clearly upset by the events of yesterday. 'How can I play out of my skin all season only for that to happen at the worst time of all? That's the worst I've ever felt on a football field'. I give Evo a hug ... well, at my height, I just about get to his chest ... and it's time for the party to move on up to the board room. To a man, the expressions are ... I'd rather not be doing this

... but to their tremendous credit, other than the international squad players Craig Cathcart and Neal Eardley, the only notable absentee is Luke Varney. There aren't too many smiley happy faces as the champagne and canapés are circulated as you may expect, but the reason for that is less obvious. Yes, the lads are disappointed not to have survived but deeper than that, they know that they are all together as a group for the very last time. Ever since this astonishing story began under Simon Grayson, the dressing room spirit has always been cited as a major factor in the club's meteoric rise. 'Larry's' departure to Leeds galvanized the lads under Tony Parkes and then Ollie arrived to seal the bond even tighter. But tonight the lads know this squad is certain to break up. Matt Gilks, Crains and Vaughny are all out of contract and, short of a massive turn around in intentions, know they're likely to have played their last game for the club. The likes of Charlie, DJ and Evo will have plenty of suitors and having had a dabble at the hardest league in the world, will be fancying another shot. Then there are the Danny Coids, Rob Edwards and Jason Euells who know their time in tangerine is up and the group is to dissipate to destinations unknown. But they've been a credit as professionals and they know they have to get through this one last emotional night together.

The players and management are clapped in to a genuinely sympathetic standing ovation and I'm in the company of the Pool media team, Canners and Baz the photographer. The meal goes well and the night's entertainment sees some of the younger lads encouraged to sing on the mic – takes some bottle, but they have a real good go. Then, no show without punch, Ollie is invited up and gives a no holds barred version of 'Love Was Made For You and Me' ending on one knee in front of Kim. Audience suitably delighted, it's time for the awards. David Vaughan virtually cleans up, picking up four trophies including, for the first time ever, a unanimous Players' Player Award. Luke Varney's big dipper against Wolves wins goal of the season and Craig Cathcart is voted Young Player of the Season. The speeches are all tear jerkers but the recipients just about manage to hold themselves together until … a special award is made to Brett Ormerod to mark his unique history making goal against Tottenham. A montage of his goals in all four divisions is interspersed with video tributes from long standing mates Danny Coid and Keith Southern before the man himself is called upon for his acceptance address. Brett tries his level best to describe his years at his spiritual home but the dam breaks and there are tears on stage – and all over a packed room.

Finally, its time for the big award, The John Schofield Trophy for the supporters' votes for Player of the Season. Matt announces the results and confirms it was an extremely close run contest between Vaughny … again … and the eventual winner and asks Ollie up on stage to present the trophy to… Ian Evatt. What a 30 hours or so for the big defender, his tears of despair at Old Trafford turning into those of joy at this accolade. In handing over the award, Ian Holloway explains the history between the two. In his first book Ollie indicated that when he was managing QPR, Evo was signed without his approval. Now the gaffer explains that having being given the Blackpool job, Evatt was the first player he spoke to and that as far as he is concerned, the big defender has improved beyond recognition from his QPR days. Matt then pops a few questions to the winner on his 'proudest moment in football.' 'What was your first reaction· when you knew Ian Holloway was in the frame for the Pool job?' Evo's response was swift … 'Oh shit, don't appoint him or that's me out of the door!' Fittingly, Evatt pays tribute to the group of players and thanks the gaffer for his part in his outstanding progress and development as a player. He departs the scene to a thunderous standing ovation and there isn't a dry eye in the house. On a night of raw emotion, there were tears aplenty – but not one was shed due to the fact the club had failed valiantly in its survivial bid against overwhelmingly impossible odds. The tears came out of the realization that a very special dressing room collective was shaking hands together as colleagues for the very last time. The tears came out of a very special bond between the players, staff and their wonderfully loyal supporters. And last but by no means least, the tears came out of the fact that this fairytale adventure had come to an end. 'This is the best trip we've ever been on!'

*

Afterword
by Ian Holloway

The ever shortening close season has given everybody time to reflect on the campaign in the sun, none more so than Ian Holloway. Just eight weeks after the final reckoning I met up with him on the night of Pool's first pre-season friendly against Rangers to look back at an astonishing season. From August right through to the end of May his over riding emotion has been pride in the achievements of his written off squad and my initial question is an attempt to establish how those emotions are now.

'I'm devastated and haunted by several key moments over the course of the season. I keep playing them over and over in my mind, they torture me and I'm convinced we got a raw deal. They say what goes around comes around...I'm still waiting! You can list them... Man City - gracious me, we were done like a kipper. Both of Tevez goals shouldn't have stood and by the number of calls I had, the whole country agreed with me that the officials should have access to technology. But nothing happens does it? Then Marlon

(Harewood)'s alleged push against Everton cost us two more points and it got worse after Christmas. Don't get me started about the (Manchester) United game, we deserved that two goal lead and then Reg (Luke Varney) gets smashed in the box, smashed he was. Even Sir Alex thought it was a pen. How could he (referee Peter Walton) wave that away and if ever a moment turned a game that was it. Dear me – I didn't think it could get worse, but then the World Cup Final referee (Howard Webb at Blackburn) had a go didn't he? That was a blatant foul on Fletch when time was up. He gives a goal kick then a free kick when Fletch never touched the lad. You just knew they would score. Lee Mason's a good referee but he knows he dropped one against Arsenal. Alright, they should have been out of sight at half-time, but if he gives that penalty we're in it again. How far away was he – five yards? Blow me it was outrageous. Then we had all that rubbish about active or passive when Van Persie finished us off – they need to sort all that out. Near the end when it was getting tight we played ever so well at Spurs only for Jermaine Defoe to strike one like that. It felt like a kick in the guts. Chis, if just one of those had gone our way, we'd be sitting here talking about something else. Alright, I know we'll have had a few iffy ones too but those big calls spoiled a fantastic effort by a group of people who deserved more.

'But having said all that it was the summer where it all went wrong. We didn't do things early enough, we didn't do things quick enough, whereas if we had that chance again we'd definitely do it now. It was a really difficult one. We were waiting for the money to come and we really needed to move the club to where those big wages had to come. Now we're back in a division which I believe will be even tougher than when we came up when you look at the teams who've come up and spent big money. The vultures have been in and picked our bones but it could have been worse, we could well have lost a few more. Varney, Puncheon as it stands, Charlie, Vaughny and probably DJ. How much tougher does it get?'

We discuss the fact that hindsight is a wonderful thing and there are doubtless many things that he would have done differently. Can he pick out the biggest of those?

'Again, it would have to be the signings in the summer. There were three that I wanted who would have made a huge difference. The Chairman and I should have been more decisive and I should have been more assertive. It was purely their wages and we were waiting for the big money to come. It didn't happen but I believe if we'd been given that chance again we'd have done it. Coming up through the play offs we were always playing catch up but we should have done the big signings...I should have stuck to my guns and now I'm furious that I didn't. That bit of extra quality would have given me the chance to pull a few people out of it when they needed a break. But the strength of the division meant that we had to be full on and right at it all the time and I knew we couldn't rotate like the rest. Such is life'.

How much does Holloway feel that losing those three successive games to freezing weather disrupted Blackpool's season?

'When it happened on the back of Stoke and Bolton we had a real momentum with us and the lads were beginning to believe in themselves as Premier League players in their own right. But it wasn't just losing the games. We couldn't train properly and work on the shape that we'd had the success with. The lads needed to do it, develop it and take it on further. But what could we do about the weather? When I took the job they told me it never snowed in Blackpool. Were they having a laugh? When we did get round to playing them we won two out of the three and we almost won the other one but what that did was to give us a back-log of fixtures that our small squad didn't cope with. We just couldn't see that we had to put bad results behind us and look how far we had come. It got to everyone. I remember Evo shouting 'That's embarrassing' in one televised match 'cos he knew people would be talking about Blackpool and what they were doing. But we should never have been in that situation. I said to the Chairman that we've stolen Sky TV's money. The team had catapulted us there and we weren't anywhere near ready. Everybody's got an under 21 squad – we haven't. Everybody's got players to put in – we hadn't. I think Arsenal's is 60. Man. Utd.'s is 73 and you can only have 25. But in the Champions League and the FA Cup you can play anyone of them so they stack 'em and rack'em. Blow me, we needed some others and we got six in the end but we didn't do it quick enough.'

It was time for me to ask the big question. How much did the transfer window disrupt you?

'I don't think you can put words on that. I think that was the beginning of the end. Heads were turned, people came in and weren't proper. Offering £1.5m for Charlie – that's where Aston Villa started. Come on! Birmingham offered that as well. We were never going to take insulting money like that. The problem is that agents know this is the time of year when they can make a killing and they don't care what damage it can do to your club. They're in the ears of their players all the time and players are bound to be unsettled by it. People talk about Charlie but he wasn't the only one I can tell you and now Charlie's got what his ability deserved. There was never a question he wouldn't get it, but we could have just done without that at the time. Personally, I don't think we needed the argument early on in the season about his extra bonus. It got Charlie angry, it got the Chairman angry, but they both thought they were right. Unnecessary really, completely unnecessary and it should never have got anywhere near court. But overall, I couldn't fault anybody for their efforts and what they achieved. I've had a look at it and I believe we need to step on now. We need to get a new squad and get some people who want to be here, full stop. People who want to be here for the right reasons, not because we've got some money, or people think we've got some money. That's not easy when there's so much money in this game. We used to do fantastically well in doing deals, the Chairman in particular, in getting unbelievable value for money. Now, everybody sees him with a huge wedge...is it £97million? It's a tad frustrating for him cos people want some of it. That's the way the game is and you're either in it or you're not. And we're certainly in it now!'

Having talked about the moments that tortured him, I ask the Gaffer about the high points of the season. Uncharacteristically, he takes a while to answer. 'I'm struggling to remember them Chis to be honest. It was so great, it was so wonderful a challenge for me as a coach and as a person to deal with these places we were going and how they did things. We were on the telly every week and even the interviews would be phenomenal. But do people realize that? I didn't take one extra interview anywhere. All I did was do my job to talk to all those people, but if you look at some of the websites, they're saying where's Ian Holloway now? Why isn't he talking to anyone? What do they want me to say...zipedee doo, we went down? Now it'll be me, you and Canners (Steve Canavan from *The Blackpool Gazette*) won't it? We're yesterday's news I'm afraid and we've got a mountain to climb. But how well did we do hey? OK so we went down in the end but we shut a few up on the way didn't we? Won't get ten points, won't win a game...that was disrespectful that was. You ask Liverpool if we were the worst team ever to play in the Premier League. Goodness me, if my dad could have seen me at Anfield. He worshipped everything that club did and just to see me on the touchline up against them...he would have been so proud. And what about the lads winning for Parky at Newcastle? That news devastated the whole place and for them to put on a show like that just confirmed what a special group they were. I felt like Dick Turpin at Sunderland but they did the same to us at home. I remember saying to you at Wigan on the first day that we had to keep our feet on the floor. The next game we got done six at Arsenal. Such is the quality you couldn't relax for a moment.'

Still on the theme of image, I try to find out how he was received by his Premier League counter-parts. 'Do you think you were respected in your own right as a Premier League coach and manager rather than for Ollieisms?' This time the response is rattled back – 'I don't know. It's like marmite, you either like it or you don't and I'm definitely one of them. I had a bit on my holiday. I went to the toilet and when I came back my wife said she'd overheard some people say that they'd recognized me and that they didn't like me. There's that Ian Holloway...I don't like him. It upset me cos they didn't even know me. Great! So I can't really answer that one. I tried to play a way that I was proud of. I stated it before I came. I tried to play and entertain and was proud of the way we stuck to it. OK, devastated when we were a tad too open at times. I need to try and correct that but the formula we had was very, very successful and I need to try and give that to other people and add to it a bit, but the dynamics ain't gonna be the same. What I'm trying to explain to the Chairman is ... how good was David Vaughan, how good is Charlie, how good is DJ.? We've lost them and it's not our fault. We're just a victim of circumstances. How good was our shape, can I get it back again? I'm gonna have to find that out. But without quality and without a balance, nothing works and what I've seen tonight against the best team in Scotland, we're way off. My other team wouldn't have been I believe. So we've got to dust ourselves down and start again and try to find some other people who can play that way or adapt what we're going to do. I'd rather find people who could do that rather than change. I'd rather be attack minded and positive like the best team in the world by a mile at the moment and that's Barcelona'.

Our conversation was gradually drifting from one of reflection to the challenges awaiting around the corner. But I couldn't let him go without reference to a controversial comment in that tension filled last week of the season. 'Following on from that, you famously said that the Premier League would be glad to see the back of you and Blackpool. Do you stand by that and is it your view that the division is set up to see the smaller clubs fail?'

'We were the smallest club ever to be in it and we failed and it was almost inevitable. But they didn't help us with their rules. They gave us their money which is fine but there's no rules on how you spend it. You need a vast array of players on big money and we couldn't do that and change the contracts of our players. That hindered me at the end of the season. Because of the Premier League rules I had to tell some people before the last game of the season who was staying and who was going and all without knowing which league we'd be in. How they wouldn't let me delay that – I'll never forgive 'em. And as for all those nice things they said about a breath of fresh air … bob off will you! What I want to say to them is the rich are getting richer and for me, how can that be sport? What matters is that the little fella should be able to beat the bigger fella and they can't see it cos those people are getting bigger all the time. Those people are also the ones who are making the rules. They're part of the decisions and that ain't fair and that can't be right and I don't like it. That's what makes it hard for clubs to break into the circle. I understand they all want to keep what they've got but it's hardly a level playing field is it? Good luck to Norwich and Swansea and QPR because they're gonna need it. They'll come up against the same as we did so they'll need it. Coming from where we did, with what we had, with our budget, I don't believe it will ever be done again. Nothing about us was anywhere near ready for what we had to do both on and off the field. But nobody can say that we didn't have a right good go can they? It was some ride Chis wasn't it?' Sure was Gaffer - 'The Best Trip'.

July 2011